transparent

transparent

Getting Honest about Who We Are

and Who We Want to Be

Sarah Zacharias Davis

Grand Rapids, Michigan

© 2007 by Sarah Zacharias Davis

Published by Fleming H. Revell
a division of Baker Publishing Group
P.O. Box 6287, Grand Rapids, MI 49516-6287
www.revellbooks.com

Printed in the United States of America

Library of Congress Cataloging-in-Publication Data
Transparent : getting honest about who we are and who we want to be / [edited by] Sarah Zacharias Davis.
    p.   cm.
    Includes bibliographical references.
    ISBN 10: 0-8007-3171-9 (pbk.)
    ISBN 978-0-8007-3171-7 (pbk.)
    1. Christian women—Religious life. 2. Self-actualization (Psychology)—Religious aspects—Christianity. I. Davis, Sarah Zacharias, 1975–
BV4527.T72 2007
248.8′43—dc22   2006038296

All epigraphs at the beginning of each chapter are taken from quotationspage.com and wisdomquotes.com

For my mother.
Gentle and generous,
she is the strongest woman I know,
and she wields her strength
to empower those she loves.

contents

7

acknowledgments

I'D LIKE TO express my earnest and enormous thanks to all the women I interviewed for this book. Many of you I had never met until we sat face-to-face. I learned so much from each one of you that there is no doubt in my mind that God wanted our paths to cross. And so I thank you for how you touched my life.

I am also grateful to Dianne Grove, Jill Carattini, Joyce Gary, and Scott Kauffmann for the authors they have introduced me to; the works of Clarissa Pinkola Estes, Marion Woodman, Annie Dillard, Sue Monk Kidd, and Anne Lamott have impacted both my thinking and my writing. I thank you, for their books have become a part of me.

Again, I want to thank Tina Jacobson and Jeanette Thomason for their encouragement and belief in the purpose of this book. I drew from your confidence and encouragement almost daily as I wrote.

Lastly, my deepest appreciation to my dear family and friends who supported me along this project; you know who you are. I can't thank you enough for that support.

introduction

thoughts about strength

SARAH

ONCE HEARD THAT if a woman is ever attacked she should drop to the ground and fight with her legs. Why? It seems like strange advice, after all, to get into the most vulnerable position—on her back—and fight her attacker from the last position she would want to be in. But, for a woman, her powerhouse of strength lies in her hips and pelvis.

Two years ago I had the opportunity to travel to India; it was my first visit to the country as an adult, and it forever changed me. There I visited the city of Varanasi, a holy city of Hinduism. It is a crowded and bustling city; the streets teem with people, carts full of produce, cows, dogs, and spiritual men. The city is

11

still very traditional and deeply rooted in its ancient culture. At dusk, we stepped into a boat and paddled out upon the famed Ganges River, and as night crept in, stealing the daylight, the darkness filled the senses in every way—the smells, the beating of drums calling to worship, the chanting. Only the imposing shadows of ancient buildings could be seen at the shore slowly sinking over time into the river. Then the taste of smoke and dirt saturated the air, and blaze after blaze dotted the night sky, filling the darkness with light and creating a haze of smoke that only added to the mysterious surroundings. The fires were funeral pyres burning the body of someone's husband or son, sister or mother. In the early morning hours, what was not yet burned would be spilled into the river, a body of water believed to be holy.

We were told by our guide that the last part of the female body to burn is the pelvic bone. That bone is often all that is dropped into the watery grave, often resurfacing to be seen by boaters or bathers. Our bones bear the last of our physicality when we have left this world; they remain, long after the flesh, a symbol of our life and strength. And the core of a woman's bodily strength is the last of her to remain, outlasting even the heat of an inferno.

Clarissa Pinkola Estes, author of *Women Who Run with the Wolves*, titled her book as such because in her study of wolves she traced a parallel between the female wolf and the woman. Without needing to give this idea too much thought, and knowing little about wolves, we could probably guess some of the parallels. Wolves are territorial, protective of their young, and travel in packs. The same could be said for women. But Estes also found similarities in their heightened sensing, their playful spirit, and their capacity for devotion. The Jungian psychologist maintains that, like wolves, women have an inherent wildness.

I began thinking about Estes's ideas. Many of our assumptions about wolves are negative. For instance, there are famous bad wolves. The one in "Little Red Riding Hood," who ate the poor, invalid grandmother, then went after Little Red Riding Hood herself. The wolf in the "Three Little Pigs" huffed and puffed and blew the poor, helpless pigs' houses down. Then there is the saying "a wolf in sheep's clothing." Not exactly a compliment.

And perhaps the idea of wildness in women has negative connotations as well. Many books have been written about the emasculation of men. But what about the taming of women? In years past, the containment of women even expressed itself in things like corsets and girdles. Women used to grow their hair long but always wore it pinned up. After a certain age it was considered immodest to let your hair hang down your back, loose and free. Hence the saying "let your hair down." To us that means "relax, be free, be yourself without worrying what others will think."

Like the wolf, we need to be wild. Not in the sense of being out of control, though at times we all probably feel that way. The wildness that exists in us as women is a fierce strength, and I think it exists because we need that strength. It is in our God-given wildness that we find our endurance, our devotion, and our fierce loyalty. All of which are a part of the beauty of our gender.

Wasn't it Eleanor Roosevelt who famously likened women to a tea bag? "We don't know our strength until we are put into hot water," she said. We all know the power of a woman, from the face that launched a thousand ships or a White House scandal, to Mother Teresa or the woman you and I know who fought back from breast cancer. But do we know our own strength? We see it in others, but do we recognize it in ourselves? Do we see the power that has been given to each one of us? And I'm not talking about the kind of power that we use to overpower another person; it's not about being top dog—or alpha wolf. It is an inner strength and intensity.

The strength of a woman takes on many different faces. And it must. Dorothy Sayers said, "Perhaps it is no wonder that women were the first at the cradle and last at the cross."[1] We could all tell story after story of tragedy and trial in the lives of many of the women we know. And yet there exists resilience and a potent energy even in the face of adversity. Even when she doubts she has anything left, she fights for her family, for those she loves, and often lastly, for herself.

And yet, there is much that has hindered women's strength. Often the dictates of culture have attempted to stifle that power, thereby creating methods of manipulation. In the film *My Big Fat Greek Wedding* there is a humorous dialogue between mother and daughter when the mother tells the daughter that though the man may be the head, the wife is the neck, turning the head as she sees fit. We laugh. And we laugh mostly because it's true—how many of us do that! But often power-tampering happens within us and is not merely the result of an outside force working on us.

I was sitting in the presence of two very beautiful women. Both were gracious and energetic and dedicated to working for the causes of women, one in Europe and one throughout Asia, and they worked tirelessly and at great personal sacrifice to themselves. As I sat in the small, IKEA-furnished living room in the heart of the city with these two women, one of them, a stunning blonde, spoke of the struggles that the women there in her charming European city wrestled with. She spoke of issues of self-esteem, searching for value from places and people who did more harm than help, and competition with other women. As the evening became late, we heard the sounds of awakening nightlife rousing outside the open window, and then the conversation turned more personal.

Each woman spoke transparently, only now about their own insecurities. I sat back in my chair and listened, taking it all in, somewhat surprised. Not because they said anything I hadn't heard other women (myself included) say before. But because these women were so beautiful, so accomplished, so giving to others, and so committed, I naively expected they wouldn't have the same insecurities of women less beautiful, less successful, and even less committed. It was an ignorant assumption, and yet there I was in my surprise. I shook my head, inwardly frustrated with all that seems to hold us back as women. And right there I got to thinking about women, and strength, and what threatens that strength. In the presence of these extraordinary women it occurred to me that we as women—as human beings—are intended for a purpose. And we all have our individual gifts that enable us to live for that purpose, whatever it is. But what keeps us from accessing that strength? What keeps us from being the most effective version of ourselves?

When I was a little girl, I couldn't wait to grow up. I spent a great deal of time imagining how wonderful it would be. As a young child, I always worried about not being pretty, about being shy, about whether or not people liked me. As I got a little older, I got jealous, always sizing myself up against the most popular girl in my class. I worried a boy would never like me and that I'd never get asked out on dates or go to the prom. I was afraid I would never be good enough. But I always thought that all the things I worried about as a young girl would magically disappear with the guaranteed wisdom that comes with age and with living more of life. And I also somehow thought this miraculous insight and life experience came at the ripe age of like, oh . . . twenty-one! But now I know, as I'm sure you do as well, that is not the case. Sure, some things do get better. Sometimes we actually get to the place where we are secure in our bodies, content in our talents, and sure of our passion and calling.

One morning I was leaving my apartment to drive to work. As I was getting into my car, I heard a little voice calling out. I looked around and noticed on the other side of the hedge a little girl calling out to me with tears streaming down her face. She asked me if the bus had already gone. I didn't know, but I recalled that I usually saw children waiting for the bus at the entrance to the complex. I told her that I thought the bus came to the front and pointed in that direction. She only looked at me, so I offered to drive her there. I didn't think she'd say yes, being that I was a total stranger, but as soon as I offered she bounded quickly around the hedge and over to my car. As I helped her in, I caught sight of her little pink backpack and a fistful of homework papers. She was still sniffling a little but had stopped crying. I asked her where she lived, and she rattled off so rapidly in Spanish I couldn't understand her. I prayed under my breath that the bus hadn't come yet, because I didn't know what I would do with this sweet little girl in my car.

As we turned the corner and approached the entrance to the complex, I saw a lot of children running around, still waiting for the bus. I exclaimed, "Look, there they are, you haven't missed the bus!" She looked at me, her face still stained with tears, and a huge smile spread across her little face. She scrambled to get out and join the other kids as quickly as she had hopped into my car. For the moment her day was made, and I, too, could have just gone home and called it a day. I felt like a superhero.

As I drove away, I couldn't help wishing that adult problems were so easy to solve. Often even when we make progress, we still have setbacks and struggle with fears. So what are the things we think about and wrestle with as women? What keeps us from being who God created us to be? And just what are the secret thoughts that plague our psyches that we never tell, or at least rarely tell?

When I thought about women and wolves it reminded me of a book I once read by Nicholas Evans titled *The Loop*. The story takes place out West in rancher territory. There are troubles with wolves wounding and killing the cattle, and so the town calls for a wolf biologist to the rescue. The biologist, Helen, believes she is there to trap the wolves only temporarily so she can record their vitals and measurements and attach a tracking device to the pack. Then armed with this information she will study their patterns and discover what is driving them to cross the line over to human territory and attack the calves. But the ranchers are realists; with each slain cow there are dollars lost, and this is their livelihood. They want the wolves dead—and quickly.

In one beautifully written scene, the wolf biologist comes across one of her traps that has ensnared a wolf in its steel talons. Helen, along with a teenage boy, Luke, who assists her in collecting the information on the wolves, hurries to check out the trap. As they near the captured wolf, they find it is none other than the alpha female of the pack. Making their way to where the wolf is held captive, they can see the wolf is large and strong with very pale, almost white fur; she is barely visible against the backdrop of the snowy wilderness. When they come close to her they see how angry she is; after all, her paw is caught in the steel trap. She lunges at them, showing her teeth and snarling, trying to break free. But the chain yanks her backward, cutting a gash in her leg and making her relatively harmless as it overpowers her ferocious force.

I'm sure you see where I'm going with this. I think that many of us, at one time or another, are much like the wolf in the snare. Strong and capable, as God has empowered and enabled us, and yet we are caught in a trap of some kind, and it holds us down, or keeps us back, even cuts us deeply to the bone, the core of our strength.

And there was something else in the story that was probably incidental and added only for aesthetic purposes and to serve as a description, but I saw further truth buried in it. As Helen and Luke saw the imprisoned alpha female up close, they saw that her fur wasn't as pale and white as they thought from afar. There was much more dimension to her beauty. She had layers, multiple layers, of brown, black, even red fur. And together the combination was beautiful and majestic.

In the pages that follow, you will read about women of all ages and experiences who have shared with candid transparency about what ensnares them, what keeps them from being the women they know they were created to be. They declare themselves to be much deeper and more complex than they may allow themselves to be seen, proving that what you first see isn't all there is. As they say, "There is more than meets the eye." They share their pasts, their present, and where they hope to be in the future. With brave honesty they share woman to woman the questions and the answers in their hearts and in their heads, and what they've both wondered and uncovered along the way. In simple declaration they are saying, "For me this is what I know, this is where I stand."

In her book *Traveling Mercies*, Anne Lamott tells of a time in her life when her son was very sick but the cause of his illness had as yet eluded his doctors. The young boy was submitted to medical test after test to determine the cause. One week while waiting for the results of another bout of tests, Anne was finding it increasingly difficult to maintain a façade of serenity in front of her young son. In her own fear and angst, she sought refuge in the bathroom away from the perceptive eyes of the little boy. (I, for one, can relate to this, having spent many moments sitting on the cold hard reality of the bathroom floor and trying to figure out my life.) Anne tells how throughout the week, friends stopped by and sat with her on the bathroom floor, comforting her, crying with her, praying with her. And Anne, seeing the therapeutic value of that honesty, of her messiness and the truth of her friendships, writes, "It would be great if we could go in and out of this place . . . but mostly it seems like we can't do it when we have our act together, because we can't do it when we're acting."[2] So I want to know, do you have a bathroom floor? What I mean is, do you have moments when your act isn't together? And with whom do you share those moments?

I think about this book as a group of women sitting on the bathroom floor. It shouldn't be that hard to imagine. We are, after all, the gender that is teased about visiting public rest-rooms in groups. Think of how many important conversations you've had with each other in the bathroom! We share the mystery, charm, and strength of our gender, and with those shared strengths come fears and insecurities common to many women. But how do we acknowledge those fears without letting them inhibit the women we were made to be? And why would we want to know the fears of other women (other than for morbid curiosity) when we have our own battles to fight? Is it because we take pleasure in someone else's pain?

No, rather it is because each woman has a story to tell. And it is my hope that you find these stories to be like bread crumbs marking your own path, reminding you of where you've been, casting the light of insight into your present, and illuminating where it is you want to go so that you find your way home. For each woman, it is a story that is her own, and we listen because as Clarissa Pinkola Estes writes, "Stories are medicine . . . they have such power, they do not require that we do, be, act, anything—we need only listen. The remedies for repair or reclamation of any lost psychic drive are contained in stories. Stories engender the excitement, sadness, questions, longings, and understandings that spontaneously bring what we need to the surface."[3] And there's another reason. Andre Dubus said that stories are what our friends tell us in their pain and joy, their passion and rage.[4]

And so here are the stories of your friends.

1

finding the courage to be me

WHITNEY

Well-behaved women rarely make history.

—Laurel Thatcher Ulrich

HAT DOES IT mean to be a Christian woman? Does being a Christian woman mean that I am one type of woman? Is there a universal mold? Do I have to have a particular look, act a certain way, speak a certain way? Can I say what's on my mind? Can I disagree with you? Can I wear Prada shoes? Ultimately, I'm asking, is it okay to be me? This is the question I struggled with for a long time. I now believe that being a woman is a wonderfully advantageous thing. After all, it seems that men are relegated to a more confined role of what is socially acceptable, but in the society in which we live now, women can be anything—and are. We have the freedom to morph between roles, and I believe a truly smart woman does so without losing who she is. In society, it's okay to be tough, to be feminine, to be a tomboy, or to take control of a situation. It's okay to be a stay-at-home mom, an attorney, an architect, or a police officer.

But I'll be honest; within Christian society women don't seem to be free to be themselves. Certain roles are not acceptable for women. As we near the possibility of the country's first female president, I say bring it on, let's have a woman as president. But I've heard many Christians, men and women alike, say they don't believe a woman should be president. Strong women are just not accepted and seem to be constantly misunderstood. Men especially don't know how to respond, and women just seem to judge them for their strength. There is no safe place for the strong-willed woman, it seems. And yet, when women are blindsided with the realities of life, as most people are at some point, it is their strength and independent spirit that enables them to persevere.

I feel that only a certain type of woman is accepted and thought to be godly. And the problem is, and has always been, that I'm just not the kind of woman that every Christian female is supposed to be. And so I've spent a lot of time trying to be someone I wasn't and trying to be the cookie-cutter Christian woman.

From the time I was a child I was a free spirit. And this didn't go over well with most people. I was kicked out of most of the childhood activities my mom enrolled me and my brother in—swimming lessons, preschool, and tennis. I was five years old, and it was Wednesday night at church. We were gathered in one of the children's classrooms that smelled like animal crackers and disinfectant. We were having snack time—which we all know is just filler time. I mean, I seriously doubt any child is famished after merely an hour of flannel-graph Bible stories. We were probably just bored, and so they fed us. The origins of emotional eating begin in Sunday school and the like, but I digress. So we were sitting at little round tables and drinking juice out of paper cups. You remember that cheap, imitation orange drink that was always served in the waxy Dixie cups. Well, rather than drinking out of the large hole in the top of the cup like every other child, I insisted on poking a hole with a pencil in the bottom and drinking from there. My teacher was not particularly keen on this idea, as I was dripping orange drink all over the table, and after several unsuccessful attempts to get me to stop, she sent me out in the hall. I occupied myself out there for a while, playing with the contents in my purse (yes, even at five I carried a purse).

After an eternity in five-year-old time, she returned to me and asked if I was ready to come back in the classroom. I only looked up at her, my lips tasty and shimmering with freshly applied pink bubblegum ChapStick, and smartly replied, "No, thank you, I like it out here." Desperate to get me under control, the teacher got down to my level and said, "*I* am the boss, you are not the boss." And putting my chubby, child hands on each of her cheeks, I leaned in, looked into her eyes with equal seriousness, and answered, "No, *you* are not the boss, God is the boss." Ah, those Sunday school lessons had served me well.

I thought my mother should have been proud of my impromptu use of biblical knowledge. But sorry to say, that night I was kindly invited not to come back, and my parents weren't exactly celebrating. No more cheap juice! Sure, I could have been disciplined for that, and maybe I would have been remorseful, but then there would have been something else, another situation, misunderstanding, or altercation. Because the thing is, I colored outside the lines. No, this isn't an excuse to do whatever you want. But I always have been that way, and my parents worked very hard to guide those lines as much as possible without crushing who I was.

I grew up with a great deal of acceptance from both my parents. My father constantly affirmed me, telling me he loved me every single day. I was taught that I could do anything I desired when I grew up. Any talents I possessed were nurtured by both of my parents. They bolstered my passion for life and always encouraged my ideas (even when many of them were doomed to fail from the beginning). For instance, when I was young, too young to travel alone, I decided I wanted to go overseas on a mission trip. My parents were hesitant because of my age but ultimately helped me work to make my dream come true.

But eventually we enter that stage where the affirmation and acceptance of our parents isn't enough and we begin to crave it from others: the dreaded stage of adolescence, when girls are twelve one minute and twenty-two the next, then revert to twelve again almost before you can blink. I began seeking approval from friends, teachers, boys, and then strangers. All of a sudden I had a need to fit in. But in my Christian high school I struggled very much with who I really was, in regard to both my personality and the way I looked. I felt a very intense pressure to be thin, blond, compliant, and meek. I was none of those things! Not only did my personality not fit, but my image didn't either. I felt judged by other Christians for how I dressed and looked. I had my own sense of style, like everything else. But the attention to detail that I gave to my appearance made me an object of more criticism.

As I got older the criticism continued. People accused me of being materialistic and made comments about how much money I spent on my clothes. They acted like I robbed poor children in Africa to sustain my shopping habit. I felt like I always needed to explain that I still tithed 10 percent and saved 10 percent before spending my money on clothes. My well-tailored clothes, coordinating jewelry, and manicured nails didn't win me any points, and sometimes I had the distinct impression a few people wanted to knock me off my three-inch heels. When I began my career plans, I said I wanted to be an interior designer. People acted like I was being shallow, and some even so much as asked what coordinating upholstery and window treatments had to do with the Great Commission. The weight of the pressure threatened to crush me and certainly buried who I was for a long time. All of a sudden the safety of my parents' acceptance wasn't enough; I was determined to earn it from everyone else. Only I struggled, as anyone would who was trying to be something they're not.

We all feel pressure to look a certain way even though in our heads we know it's unreasonable and even wrong. In those all too rare moments when we're honest with ourselves and with each other, we admit the pressure is there and we even denounce it. We acknowledge with occasional clarity that those models on the covers of magazines are airbrushed, that those actresses can devote all their time, and money, into getting fit after a baby, and that the average woman isn't five foot ten and 115 pounds. I don't mean to make light of the burden of that often unobtainable physical image—we can destroy ourselves with it. And many women do, even risking their lives. But it is also generally accepted that the pressure to meet one physical standard of beauty is just inherently wrong—and impossible besides—and therefore there is no shortage of support when we need a little reassurance.

There is a general consensus among women that those expectations are wrong. But what about the pressure to have a certain type of personality? The same pressure exists, but without the readily available support. Growing up, I read devotional book after devotional book that talked about the traits of a godly woman. Words like *submissive*, *feminine*, *quiet*, and *meek* were used. And then there were verses like 1 Peter 3:3–4: "Your beauty should not come from outward adornment . . . instead it should be that of your inner self, the unfading beauty of a gentle and quiet spirit." (That verse is a loaded arsenal—they get me on multiple counts there.) Or 1 Timothy 2:11: "A woman should learn in quietness and full submission." Then there were sermons about Mary and Martha. Mary was the teachable and gentle one, and Martha, well, she argued with Jesus. The message was that we should be "Marys" and not "Marthas."

So there it was, in the Bible. Still other books talked about outspoken women and characterized those who like to take control as negative and unfeminine, contrary to the way women were designed by God to be. Many of the Christian women I spent time with modeled this too. Some seemed to take a backseat role in their own lives, letting their husbands make all the decisions without taking an active role. Rather than taking a job with any seriousness, some bided their time until their husbands agreed it was time for children. Being loud and hanging with the boys wasn't ladylike, and most never disagreed or questioned men, even if they were in the workplace and positioned in authority over a man. But I'm not criticizing them. The problem was me. I felt like the odd one out. I didn't fit in to all that.

The real me is loud at times, and sure, maybe even bossy. I'm not shy or quiet, I like nice things, I love clothes and shoes and makeup, I am strong and can take control in a situation if I see a need, I am often opinionated, and I get manicures every other week. But it felt like people seemed to overlook the other contributions I made and only criticized the perceived nonconformist side of who I was. I struggled to find some other costume to put on so that I could be accepted. But it was painful. It's crushing to feel unacceptable. People's judgments of me seemed so unfair. And so I hurled myself into self-doubt, self-obsession, and as a result self-hatred. All the while here I was trying to develop my relationship with a God who, if I believed what people were telling me, didn't accept me the way he made me. Something didn't add up about that.

And so I began to explore what Jesus really taught about the way we should be, and what he really thought about women. I think it's a necessary step for everyone who is raised in a Christian home to really take a look at their faith. You have to examine many of the things you were taught somewhere along the way and look at them closely. You can't simply adopt the faith of your father and mother; at some point you must make it your own.

What I discovered about Jesus changed everything. I think Jesus colored outside the lines too. I like what Dorothy L. Sayers said about him. She says it more profoundly than I ever could.

> They had never known a man like this man—there never has been such another. A prophet and teacher who never nagged at them, never flattered or coaxed or patronized; who never made arch jokes about them, never treated them either as "The women, God help us!" or "The ladies, God bless them!"; who rebuked without querulousness and praised without condescension; who took their questions and arguments seriously; who never mapped out their sphere for them, never urged them to be feminine or jeered at them for being female; who had no axe to grind and no uneasy male dignity to defend; who took them as he found them and was completely unself-conscious.[5]

The closer I looked, the more I saw that Jesus spent time with some pretty radical women. Jesus himself came from the line of Rahab, who was a prostitute and a pretty gutsy woman. But there was more. The woman described in Proverbs 31, who is widely considered a pretty amazing woman, wears nice clothes. That's right. She "clothes herself in fine linen and purple garments." And Esther! Ever since I was a little girl I've been fascinated with Esther because she was one of the few women in the Bible who was described as being beautiful. And she was a queen—and every little princess dreams about becoming a queen. After King Xerxes had a falling-out with his current queen, he decided to do a kingdom-wide search for a new one. Esther was brought in as a candidate simply because of her beauty. She spent the first year in the harem preparing her body to meet the king. Basically her first year at the palace was like a yearlong spa treatment! Afterward she was brought before the king, and he liked her—he liked her so much he made her queen.

But also during this time, one of the king's very own men was plotting to kill the Jews. He had even manipulated King Xerxes to sign off on the edict. Esther heard of the plan from her uncle, who pleaded with her to use her influence. But the king had a rule at that time. No one could approach him unless summoned by him. The king carried a scepter, and if he pointed one end at you, then you could come forward and your presence would be welcomed, but if he pointed the other end . . . well, then, you would be put to death immediately. But Esther was very strong and undoubtedly gutsy. She put her life on the line to save her people, the Jews. She went before the king and invited him to dinner. And she was received well because the king thought she was very beautiful. But she had brains too. She strategized and carried out her plan with methodical precision—all the time at great personal risk to herself. But she used her beauty, her strength, and her wisdom to literally change her world for the better.

I'm not saying we should become so gender neutral that we deny the feminine traits that are rightly ours; I'm not saying we behave like men; and I'm not saying we justify shallowness and outright materialism. And I'm not saying that to shrug and say "That's just who I am" is a viable excuse for sinning. Surely, whether you are male or female, you should not be unkind, rude, or disrespectful. All I'm saying is that being a woman doesn't have to look the same all the time. I'd rather be held to a human standard, not a standard for only females. After all, life is made far more interesting by an eclectic combination of personalities and life experiences. And quite honestly, without the variety, life would be boring, would it not?

For me this was the most emancipating discovery—to be free to be the woman I really am, who I was created to be. And to know that I am loved and accepted by God in all my uniqueness. That knowledge has given me the confidence to be the woman I truly am. Sure, I make mistakes, I have to apologize, and sometimes you may not always like me. You might think I spent too much money on my new Marc Jacobs platform heels that just arrived from the spring line. You might think I'm too strong or that I voice my opinion too readily, but that's okay. Because I've come to a place where I believe if I'm good enough for God, then I am good enough for everyone else. And I know he's still working on me, so you don't need to worry. It was a long path to get to where I am today. But this is who I am, and I really believe that it would be wrong not to live according to that reality. That assurance, that knowledge has set me free to be the person God intended.

Discussion Questions

1. Do you think there is a profile for the ideal Christian woman?
2. What do you think it means to be feminine?
3. How do you react to women who are different than you? Where do you think this reaction comes from?

2

living with intention

GAIL

*Autumn is a second spring when every leaf
is a flower.*

—Albert Camus

TOOK A WALK the other day in my neighborhood. It's October, and the leaves are falling. I reveled in the sound of crunching leaves under my feet as I walked. Then a car drove by, and the gust it created launched the leaves into a dance across the street. I watched as the wind scattered them about, their scent wafting under my nose, making the air smell like autumn. One small, vibrant red leaf caught my eye as it was carried away in the flurry. It turned and spun and was lifted away until I could no longer see it, as if the leaf was in search of independence and adventure, leaving the rest behind. For a moment I contemplated where it would land—whose street, whose yard. Would anyone else notice it? I wondered how far it would be carried if it survived until the end of the season without being stabbed mercilessly by a rake and scooped into someone's trash bag to sit on the curb. An unsettled feeling threatened my pleasant mood as for a moment I imagined myself as that leaf, tossed so easily by the power of a gust of wind.

I really don't feel like I have much power as a woman. Or I guess I never really thought about it. I think of other women as having power. An accurate portrayal of that power is in the movie *Steel Magnolias*, in which women are portrayed as not only loving and nurturing but also strong and enduring. They survive illness, unfulfilling marriages, childbirth, even the death of a loved one. Yes, they are perhaps physically weaker than men, but they are tougher and able to withstand stress far better.

But I don't feel I have the power that I see in other women. I don't feel as if I'm made out of steel; I'm more like that red leaf carried away on the whim of an autumn breeze. Or like the feather in *Forrest Gump*, floating in and out of scenes in someone else's movie. I feel that rather than being grounded, sure, and intentional, I am lifted and carried by the events of my life without a say in where I go or what I do. I guess I feel this way because none of my life today is what I dreamed it would be. Sure, I have some of the outward markings of success, but inside I feel lost. I feel like the old Frosted Flakes commercial that used to run when my kids were young. The adult is portrayed as serious and responsible, saying they like a healthy breakfast, then a child version of the same person says they like the crispy frosted flakes. Outside I appear like a successful, self-assured adult of fifty, but inside I am a child still very unsure of my next move.

I was one of five children, and I was the youngest girl. I had an older sister, and we looked so much alike—only everyone thought she was prettier. Not only that, but I always felt like she was better than me at all the activities we both participated in—piano lessons, ballet, choir. And worse, I knew our parents thought she was better too. No matter how much I tried to achieve, no matter my success, I always felt trapped in her shadow. She sang better, played the piano better, did better in school—everything seemed to come easy to her. I felt unimportant and insignificant to my family and to the rest of the world. But I learned to do what was necessary to feel accepted.

I began to intuitively read people and sense what they expected of me, then I would try to fit their expectations. I aimed to please as my ticket into their sphere of acceptance, even appreciation. Somehow I have put up a good act of confidence and strength. But it is just that, an act. I didn't set out to exude quiet confidence, and I'm not sure how I pulled

it off, but somewhere along the way people started assuming
that my quietness and the mysteriousness I conveyed was
strength and self-assurance, though it couldn't be farther from
the truth. And yet I keep up the image and play into that
idea; I allow people to think that way about me. I make it a
point never to let them see anything that could be perceived
as weakness.

I don't tell them who I really am. And, I guess, why would I?
Oh, there are times when I want to shed my tough outer skin.
In a moment of wanting to be known I reveal the desperation
underneath. And each time, people respond with shock, which
is not the reaction I want. I want sympathy or empathy, not
disappointment. Often in my friendships I am the spiritual
advisor, the mother, the grown-up. People come to me with
their problems, and I listen and advise. And people get used to
that pattern. We get into roles in relationships, and once a dy-
namic is established it's hard to change. I take on the caretaker
role, often not even intentionally, and then inevitably when
I show my frightened self in a moment of weakness, when I
ask questions I don't have answers to, I am met with rejection
and disappointment. Once a friend actually reprimanded me,
telling me I was the spiritual one, I was supposed to have all
the answers, to be strong and set the example for others. But
sometimes I wish I could cast off that persona even though it
has brought me such success. I wish I were free to fall apart,
and I wish someone would catch me, but instead everyone is
depending on me, and I choose every day to live up to that
expectation.

Somewhere along the way I learned what I had to do. I learned how to play the game, and I guess in some ways it has worked for me. For example, I never wanted a career; I wanted a large family and a big home full of laughter and memories where my children could grow up. I'd spend the day making chocolate chip cookies and chicken potpies. I envisioned all my children's friends coming to play at our house, even wanting to stay for dinner. We'd have a crowded table at family meals every night. During the holidays the house would be full of merriment, and then someday my grown children would return toting their own children. I know it sounds like a scene from the Waltons, but it was my dream.

And while I did get married, and I did have children, it didn't look a thing like the Waltons. To begin with, we did not have the large family home I wanted; we often had to scrape to get by and just make do. I had to work to help support the family. And I did this all but kicking and screaming. As it turned out, joining the workforce as an unwilling party, not caring about my career and even being angry and bitter that I had to get a job at all, was perhaps the key to my success. I just didn't care about the job because I didn't want to have one in the first place. It was not part of my dream. And so I nailed job interviews, I voiced my opinion loudly, I spoke my mind to my boss, not caring about the consequences. But people stood up and took notice of me. And I advanced quickly. I was offered a hand up by people of influence at the top who saw something in me, believed in me, and I have done well, better than I ever could have imagined. They think I'm smart, clever, mysterious, and confident. But I don't see myself as earning this success; like the feather in *Forrest Gump*, I was merely lifted to a place where I could be in the right place at the right time. I will admit that I don't think God works for good in my life, only the lives of others. And I have thought that for as long as I can remember. Even when I'm touched by God's blessings, I feel it isn't me who is being blessed but rather my husband, or one of my children, or my sister.

When my daughter was little she used to watch the Disney version of *Sleeping Beauty*. There are three fairies in the movie, each with her signature color, and that particular hue surges from her wand when she casts her spell. But the fairies get into a tiff one day and disagree on what magical intervention is needed to remedy a particular situation. As each one is sure that she is right, they try to outdo each other with the spells they cast. The fairies end up darting all over the room, waving their wands about and casting spells every which way. And when the fight has left them worn out and depleted, the room is painted like one of those tie-dyed T-shirts, color every which way. And so I feel that when faced with blessing or success I was merely splattered by a wayward wand. Funny thing is, when things go wrong, I think it was a direct and intentional hit.

But what would happen if I didn't meet people's expectations? What would happen if I believed God cared for me? Not just humanity in general, not merely his children collectively, not even my family as a whole, but actually me—with no façade, no poker face or the pretense of confidence? What would happen if I tried to make things happen for myself? What would happen if I stopped being the feather and became an arrow shot with purpose and expertise from a master archer? What if instead of being carried by life, I lived with purpose and aspiration?

Although I may appear successful, I have many dreams that I never pursued simply because I was too afraid to try. And I guess part of me never bothered because I thought any contribution I could make someone else would do better. And so though I want to blame other people, unfair circumstances, and just life in general for my shattered dreams, there were times when I just simply didn't try because I was afraid. I wanted to be a dancer, I wanted to be a writer, I wanted to sing professionally, I wanted to be a speaker. And at times I had opportunity, but I didn't seize it, I didn't live life intentionally. Because maybe I thought if I was just a feather, if I failed or didn't get to where I wanted to be, it wouldn't be my fault. It would be the fault of the wind that carried me. And that would be easier to live with.

But it isn't. And now at my age I almost don't know how to change the way I think and the way I live. Many of these ideas, these fears and insecurities, have been residing inside my head for as long as I can remember. I just don't know if I can live any differently. And yet, I don't stop dreaming even if it is too late for some of my desires. And maybe that's something. Maybe if we don't have any dreams at all, we're in a far more treacherous place than merely being disappointed that our dreams aren't realized. I have done some volunteer work with troubled children, and often I will ask them what they want to do when they grow up. My heart breaks for the children who have no answer to give. For I think even the most absurd aspiration is better than none at all. I think the absence of dreams reveals the absence of hope—and we all need hope.

And so I know what I could do; I could take small steps.

Eleanor Roosevelt once said, "Do one thing every day that scares you." I could do little things that scare me, and then maybe that will give way to bigger things. To begin with, I could try a new kind of food that I think I may not like. Or I could take dance lessons. At my age it's too late to be a professional dancer, but I could at least learn to dance. I could join the choir at my church. I could write an article and try to submit it to a magazine. I could try to find teaching opportunities. And maybe I could capture that feather once and for all. If I did finally seize it, I'd press it between the pages of my disappointments and departed dreams, where it would remain grounded forever.

When I was a little girl I used to love walking to school when it was very windy outside. I'd stand still and lean into the wind, tempting it to knock me over. It never did. Maybe one day I will stand into the wind, my legs planted firmly to the earth, my arms stretched wide, and then I'd just dare it to move me.

Discussion Questions

1. How far do you think we should go to realize our dreams?
2. What do you think is the purpose of dreams and aspirations? Are those different than goals?
3. Do you think your dreams need approval?

3

knowing my voice

RACHEL

*Put your ear down close to your soul
and listen hard.*

—Anne Sexton

REBA MCENTIRE SANG a song called "The Greatest Man I Never Knew" about a wonderful yet distant father. When Bob Carlisle released "Butterfly Kisses" I think it was played for every father-daughter dance in every wedding I went to that year. John Mayer sang about the power of a father to affect his daughter in her relationships far into adulthood. And the movie *Father of the Bride* still makes me cry regardless of the fact I've seen it about twenty-five times!

There is no disputing the special relationship between fathers and daughters, though often greater attention is given to the relationship between father and son. But fatherly affection, telling a daughter she is beautiful and creating a standard for how she should be treated, is important. I believe a daughter's relationship with her father leaves her either walking with a limp or brandishing a hidden power the rest of her life.

I love my father immensely. And I believe he is one of the greatest men in the world. He is wise, kind, compassionate, and funny. His eyes shine—always. They sparkle with laughter, or glisten with sadness or tiredness. When I was a little girl, if I was sad or afraid and my dad told me everything would be okay, I believed him. I used to sit in his lap with my head against his chest, listening to the vibration of his voice as he spoke. And I held his hand when we walked; it made me feel safe and cared for. He put me to bed every night and read to me before I slept. He told me he'd always wanted a little girl, so I knew I was special. When I was older and began to date, I measured every man against him. And no matter how old I get, his approval means everything to me. When he puts words of encouragement to paper in a letter or birthday card, I read them over and over. For him to say he is proud of me is the thing I seek in all that I do. No matter what others say, it is his opinion that carries great weight. When he is displeased with me, it cripples me. And therein lies my difficulty. I allow myself to be paralyzed and immovable when making decisions that he may not agree with. I judge every choice against what he would have me do, and when he is not in agreement with me I am in agony. As much as I love my father, I believe I have hindered myself from behaving as an adult.

When I was a child, all I wanted was to be grown up. Being an adult just seemed so glamorous. I could pick my own clothes, stay up late, get married. I always watched my mother get dressed for a party or dinner with friends, and she'd lean close to the mirror when she stroked mascara on her lashes, and press her lips together after gliding lipstick across her mouth. I couldn't wait to be just like her, wearing makeup, an elegant dress, and high-heeled shoes as she left for a night of dinner and dancing with my father.

But growing up is a whole lot harder than I envisioned as a child. It involves the bills, the responsibility, the full-time job, and having other people depend on you. How do I grow up and—to take a phrase author Marion Woodman used to title her book—"leave my father's house"? I left his house a long time ago physically; I haven't lived there for a number of years. But how do I make a choice that I believe is right for myself and not see the disappointment in his eyes when it is something other than what he would have me do? And how do I learn to trust my own voice when it speaks differently than his? How do I keep from still being that little girl twirling and twirling, calling out, "Daddy, Daddy do you see me dance?"

What would happen if I were to make my choices independently? I think it comes down to knowing when to listen to the right voice and how to blend all the voices together. I

would have to trust my own voice and the knowledge I have
been given, and I would have to know God's voice and what
he is saying.

Trusting my own voice is something that frightens me—and
hinders me. Even with the life experience I have gained I don't
know how to listen to what I know. I question how I would
know better than so many older and wiser than me, others
with more life experience or greater faith. Perhaps I don't even
know the sound of my own voice, or that which we call "gut" or
intuition. Of course, many people scoff at the idea of listening
to their gut. I remember I once told a friend to listen to her
gut, and she looked at me like I'd said something heretical.
I think as Christians we know we're supposed to hear from
God, and so we reject the idea of listening to our gut, thinking it unspiritual. But I wonder if actually God speaks to us
through that sense of intuition. I'm not suggesting we listen
to ourselves rather than God, but I think that sometimes he
speaks through our own voice. I believe that our bodies enable
us to interpret the world around us, even that which is not so
obvious, and I believe it is part of the wonder with which we
were created.

Women especially have this heightened sense of intuition.
The Gospel of Mark tells of a woman who came and broke
an expensive bottle of perfume over Jesus' feet. Jesus was eating at the home of Simon in Bethany. Reclining at the table
with Jesus were the disciples and perhaps some other men as
well. The woman approached Jesus, knelt down, and broke the
bottle. The fragrance of the perfume filled the entire house.

Then in an emotionally raw moment, she leaned her head in closer to his feet, and she began to wipe them with her long hair. The other men present looked on with utter disdain, even verbalizing their judgment of her. They began to murmur to each other in indignation over what was happening and finally severely rebuked the woman, saying to Jesus that the money she spent on the expensive bottle of perfume could have bought food for the poor. I'm sure they thought if they focused on the needs of the poor as the root of their disapproval, Jesus would be sure to back them up. Jesus cared about the poor, after all; that much they all knew. And defending the poor is always a worthy cause.

But Jesus didn't back them up. Instead he rushed to the woman's defense and admonished the men. He told them that what she had done was beautiful to him, and it was this woman who knew the death that awaited him. Her actions said that she understood what was coming, and she did all that she could—she was preparing his body for burial. Jesus even went on to say that her memory would be honored wherever the gospel was preached. It must have taken great courage to do what she did. To be openly disparaged by a room full of people—full of men—would be humiliating. I can only imagine how I would have felt. How do you think she knew what these other men hadn't realized? I think it was her intuition; it was her gut sense that told her there was more happening with Jesus than was immediately apparent. She listened to her gut, and she honored him in that way, surely knowing the other men would at the very least be puzzled by her behavior.

49

But as Christian women we often aren't aware of our intuition, or we don't trust it. Our bodies are powerful beings that speak volumes to us if we only pay attention. Once, while getting a facial at a day spa, I noticed a diagram on the wall. It was a drawing of the face and all the things that the skin on your face could communicate to you about the rest of your body, if you only took notice. A breakout on the skin along the side of the face indicates a hormonal imbalance; a breakout along the chin reveals stress. A yellow tone in your skin could mean kidney problems; another area of the face suggests indigestion. It amazed me that my face alone could expose much of what is occurring in my entire body! But while we spend plenty of time working on our bodies, exercising, dieting, and making improvements, we don't just listen.

Paula Reeves writes that Carl Jung warned "when a culture loses contact with the divine the desire to relate to the Ineffable is carried by the body as a disease." She explains his statement this way: "Inevitably, when we ignore what matters most to us that then becomes the matter within us." Paula also says, "She who knows little of her body knows less still of her soul."[6] Within your soul lies the sound of your own voice, and often we don't know how to recognize it because we don't learn to pay attention to it. Again, I'm not saying we do this rather than listen to the voice of God, but I am saying that maybe God uses that very thing—the sound of our own voices—to speak to us.

What is your "gut" or intuition exactly? The dictionary defines intuition as "perceiving of truth of something immediately without reasoning or analysis; a hunch; an insight."[7] I think intuition is different than a conscience. I think it's really an additional God-given sense that we often don't listen to. And I think that it is both very female and very powerful. And I think to know my own voice means I have to know who I really am. It means breaking through the clutter of other voices—those of my father, my mother, my friends, my pastor—all voices that are very important to me and yet voices that are not mine, or God's.

Then I think I often don't recognize the voice of God. Okay, there, I admitted it. It feels shameful, and I can never bring myself to say that out loud. And you probably think I'm un-spiritual. I've often had people tell me about times when God told them things. What house to buy, what job to take, or what to do with their life. One woman, in an attempt to encourage me in the throes of a difficult decision, spoke of her own experiences, enlightening me with example after example of how God spoke to her and so obviously moved in her life. I was stirred by what she told me but left her presence with my insides churning, feeling somewhat jealous and very much rejected by God. Why hadn't he done the same for me, especially when I was begging him for some sort of sign? Later I was able to look at the situation differently, if only in a brief moment of clarity.

I think it's wonderful that God moved so mightily and evidently in her life, but that just isn't how it has been for me. For whatever reason, God has chosen to deal with me differently. I've heard countless stories of others who didn't hear from God; rather they felt only silence in response to their earnest pleas. But finally they got something, a sign, a circumstance, something that said to them, "I'm here and I am with you." And something that seemed so obscure all of a sudden became cogent. But I don't really have those stories. I am still waiting for lucidity, and it seems like I've been waiting for years. And if God is speaking to me, then I just don't know how to evaluate what he is telling me. It's like I'm looking for signs everywhere, and then when I get one, I'm not sure if it is what I think it is.

Last spring, I was catching the red-eye from Long Beach back to the East Coast. On the way to LAX, I was riding the Super Shuttle van and sitting next to a stranger. He too was taking the red-eye home to Orlando. We struck up a casual conversation in the twenty minutes to the airport. You know the kind—what sort of work do you do, are you married, do you have kids. He asked me if I was going to work the next day even though I was missing a whole night of sleep, and I replied ruefully that indeed I was. He commented that I was a workaholic, like him. I responded that I figured if I could only have an empty seat next to me on the plane then I could sleep across it and be ready to work when I landed at six in the morning. He told me, a bit sheepishly, that he was flying first class so it wouldn't be a problem for him to sleep.

When the blue van dropped him at his terminal, we said the polite good-byes, and then he added, "I'll pray that you get an empty seat beside you." I laughed and said, "Thanks." He again said, "No, I'm serious, I will pray for that." Again

I thanked him and then thought to myself, *Don't waste your time, mister. God isn't in the habit of rushing to answer my prayers, and I don't think an empty airline seat is on the top of his list. Oh, and if he is going to answer my prayers, the empty seat isn't at the top of my list either.*

After checking in for my flight, showing my ID three times, being barked at in the security screening line while I hobbled barefoot to the other side, and purchasing my dinner of McDonald's French fries and a Coke, I settled into a chair in the waiting area at my gate. As I sat for the next thirty minutes, person after person gathered in the area. It was filling up. With every arrival it looked less and less likely I'd get my empty seat. About fifteen minutes before boarding, the gate agent began to make repetitive announcements that the plane was full, therefore the overhead bin space would be sparse and only two carry-ons were permitted, and there would be no room for standby passengers. I laughed a cynical, know-it-all chuckle to myself and shook my head. It figured. There would definitely be no empty seat.

I even thought to myself, *God, the one thing I ask for . . . is it too much to ask . . .* But that wasn't even true; I asked for many things from God. Not getting them hadn't stopped me from asking—at least not yet. So we boarded the plane, and of course it was full. But when everyone had boarded, when every passenger was seated, there was one, lone empty seat on the whole plane—next to me. I even stood up and surveyed the plane to make sure of that fact. Yes, the plane was completely full. I couldn't believe it. Was it God, or coincidence? As soon as we were airborne, I unbuckled my seat belt and contorted my body so that it could fit horizontally across two seats, and I slept almost the whole flight, waking just in time to see one of the top ten sunrises of my life—sunsets and sunrises always make me feel God's presence. All in all, Delta had been quite the spiritual experience that day.

As I drove away from the airport and headed for my office, I contemplated. Maybe it was God. Maybe it was God saying, "I know it's hard, but you have to walk this path for a while. I gave you that empty seat to remind you that I am involved in your life." But maybe that's just what I wanted it to mean. Maybe I so wanted to hear from God, I wanted that empty seat to mean something more than dumb luck. Maybe it was just an empty seat.

Ulysses "Everett" McGill is portrayed by George Clooney in the movie *O Brother, Where Art Thou?* Based on Homer's work *The Odyssey*, it tells the story of three ex-cons who escaped together, but only because they were chained together. As the other men find God along the way, Everett, the resident philosopher and religious cynic, mocks them. All through the movie there is talk of an inevitable dam break that will cause a flood, and so the men are acting on a schedule set by the impending flood. After a long series of random events the three men are about to be put to death by law enforcement officers who have finally recaptured them, and three nooses hang in wait. In desperation Everett drops to his knees and asks God to rescue them. He offers bargain after bargain, promising God this and that if God will only save them from inevitable death.

At the very second he finishes his prayer, the floodwaters barrel in and sweep the men away. Thinking quickly, they manage to stay afloat by using arbitrary items also carried by the water, and they are saved. When one of the men claims salvation from God and answered prayer, Everett quickly corrects him, saying it was the floodwaters that rescued them, giving God not another thought.

Sometimes I'm afraid I'm like Everett McGill, so obviously missing the hand of God when it is right in front of my face. And then sometimes I'm afraid if I ever do see what I perceive as a sign, I'll be one of those people who are sure everything is a sign from God. Those people get on my nerves sometimes. And often, I think they're reading into things. I once had a friend who prayed for parking spaces. And it actually seemed to work. Does God seriously care about empty seats on an airplane or good parking spaces? Maybe I'm just envious that it doesn't seem to happen that way for me. But why does it seem that God will fix something like a broken air conditioner and not heal my best friend's cancer?

I know there is no shortage of prescribed methods for hearing God, and I've tried many of them. "Pray and listen" . . . well, as I said, often—no, if I'm truthful I'd say most of the time—I just don't hear anything.

"Read the Bible" . . . well, time and again that doesn't shed light on my situation; many times it's just not that black and white. And when I read the Bible looking for guidance, I wonder if every verse I read is supposed to be a sign in some way. And if it's comfort I'm looking for, sometimes I just want something really personal. Not something between David and God, or Job and God, I want something between me and God. It's important to read the Bible, of course, but in my limited understanding, the Bible often doesn't give me the answers I'm looking for. But maybe it's because I'm closed minded where God is concerned, sure that I know what he should do or how he will respond. And so I search for something, assuming I know exactly what I'm searching for.

"Seek wise advice" . . . well, even wise people can be wrong. And their experiences may not mirror my own. So you see, often when I am searching for the answers, I come up short, and many times it's easier to find what *not* to do rather than what *to* do.

I've asked other people who seem to hear from God on a regular basis how to know what God is telling me, and the answer is "you just know." Well *I* don't. But I think it's not that I don't know God; rather it is that I think I put forth my own ideas of what I think God wants or what he will do. And I am learning that it is so often not what I expected him to do. And then when I make the choice I think may be right, and it doesn't turn out the way I thought, I question my decision making and deciphering of God's will. Even though I know in my head that something going not as planned, or even seemingly awry, does not at all represent a failed choice. So many things just seem ambiguous when I want them to be obvious. I wish that God would make things crystal clear and lead me so that I know exactly what I am supposed to do without question. I know, who doesn't want that, right?

But then I think if that were reality, if that were how it is, then life would be pretty simple. Because I'd always know exactly what to do, and if things didn't turn out the way I wanted or expected, I would still know it was part of some greater plan. But instead I am sitting in a great murky pool of ambiguity, and for some reason God often leaves me there to mull over his mystery. I have come to conclude that God is very mysterious. And that we are supposed to just live in that reality. Perhaps it is like Ruth Tucker puts it in her book *God Talk*: "Is there perhaps another perspective: one that offers a deeper comprehension and confidence in God than those that are dependent on subjective and individualized testimonials of divine intervention and communication?"[8]

We constantly try to filter everything through our special Christian decoder. But, really, I think we have no hope of demystifying the God who said, "For my thoughts are not your thoughts, neither are your ways my ways" (Isa. 55:8). It's just so hard to live in that mystery—in that ambiguity. I find myself saying, "God, if I could just get my arms around who you are, what you are and what you want, then I would know what to do." And once, as I was saying that, I closed my eyes and had a vision of me with my arms encircled around this mysterious being. My mind was focused on me (and as I say that, I wonder if perhaps that focus is part of my problem too) and the image of me with my arms encircled. And then I realized that if my arms are encircled and wrapped around something then they are closed. If they are closed, then nothing can get out, but nothing can get in either. What if rather than trying to "get my arms around God," I hold them wide open? Closed, I am not open to anything outside that circle, not open to something that God may do that I don't expect. But in that gesture of openness I am open to God's incomprehensibility. And I am open to anything God might do or not do. But then again, how do I know what that is? How do I know when the voice is God's? Maybe it is true that I will just know.

But I know enough, and I have discovered enough about God and learned enough about myself that the time has come for me to move. I think sometimes God just expects you to work with what he's given you, what you do know, even if it doesn't look like what everyone else around you seems to know. So where do I go? Where do I live if I move out of my father's house? Even with the best of intentions, I may live in a mansion of disappointment, in a house of regret, or in a shack of broken dreams. But do I really think that God will abandon me? Do I actually believe that if I go out on my own, God will not continue to guide and direct me? Do I not believe that he would still be my Father? Maybe I'm afraid to go out on my own because the reality is that God my Father will let me wallow. He'll let me live in pain, and he won't hurry to rescue me the way my earthly father will. To live in my earthly father's house is safe. But God, well, he's just not. Like C. S. Lewis's Aslan, and according to Mrs. Beaver, "He's good, but he's not safe."

But in the end I guess I could live in my own house, whatever that looks like. Because until I learn to make my own choices with responsibility and deliberateness, I won't be living my life. I'll be living someone else's. And the truth is, none of us want that. Not my father, not me, and not God. When I stand before God, it is I who must account for my life. My father won't be there to take responsibility for my choices, good or bad. While my father is very wise and I may often seek his advice, my decisions are ultimately my own. And so is the responsibility for my choices. And that means I can't lay blame or make excuses.

I don't know yet if I'm ready to move out of my father's house. I know I should and I know I will and I have packed a few bags, but I still live there. And I'll keep packing, keep growing, and soon I'll be leaving.

But I think I'll always keep a toothbrush there. Do you think that's okay?

Discussion Questions

1. How do you determine what is the right decision for you to make?
2. How do you think God speaks to you?
3. Why do you think God sometimes seems silent? What do you base your answer on?

4

jealousy

JESSICA

One need not be a chamber to be haunted;
One need not be a house;
The brain has corridors surpassing material
place.

—Emily Dickinson

HATE GENDER GENERALIZATIONS. You know, all women are this, all men are this . . . I don't like them because I think they put people in a box, forcing them to fit into social confines, or statistics, or studies, rather than just who they are. I know plenty of people, both men and women, who don't exhibit many of the traditional traits of their respective genders. That said, I know there are differences. I once heard someone say he knew gender differences existed when he had a son. Trying to be gender inclusive, he and his wife provided their son with both typically male and typically female toys, like trucks and dolls. But the difference between their son and the little girls he sometimes played with was that while the girls cradled and cooed to their dolls, he banged his doll's head against the side of a table.

So I will say that I think one of the coolest things about women is the mystery and emotional depth they often have. I remember when I was in high school, and my best friend went away for the entire summer. I was always close to my older brother, who was home from college, and he let me hang out with him and his friends a few times. I came away from spending time with them wondering what boys actually talk about. It seemed like everything they talked about really amounted to nothing. Mostly they just made crude comments about girls. Though I was still young, had I been with my girlfriends we would have talked about a deluge of things, from the fight I got into with my mom that morning and how it made me feel, to the boy I was obsessed with but whose attention I couldn't seem to capture, to spirituality, to how nervous I was about my upcoming summer job interview, to the poem I wrote the night before when I was thinking about the boy I was obsessed with.

I love the depth that we as women can tap into. And I love the mysteriousness too; with many men, it seems that what you see is usually what you get, whereas with women you often don't know exactly what they're thinking. Even Sigmund Freud said, "Despite my thirty years of research into the feminine soul, I have not been able to answer the great question that has never been answered: what does a woman want?"[9] I know that drives men crazy, but I think it makes us exciting. And I think I find this mystery fascinating because I value my own sense of intuition, my ability to read between the lines of mystery and ambiguity. I believe it is one of my personal strengths—and it is a strength that we as women share. My ability to sense the unseen, not in some mystical, supernatural way, but a gut-level knowledge that enables me to sense things, to access something else going on that is not so obvious to men, has made me good at my relationships and my job, and I have come to count on it.

But the combination of both those strengths, the depth with my intuition, creates a force within me that I often can't control. Because of my confidence that I am always attuned to more than what appears to be happening at the surface, I have become suspicious, always sure there's an angle. The Bermuda Triangle, the perfect storm, the Achilles' heel, call it what you may. What it boils down to is intuition run amuck that has ravaged its way like a wildfire through my relationships. In a word, it is jealousy—a jealousy that results from reading too much into situations. In my relationships I am always sure there is something going on that I am trying so hard not to miss. And it is really a jealousy that is out of control.

Sure, a lot of women are jealous. We covet each other's clothes, shoes, accessories, homes, and bodies. We check each other out, evaluating how we measure up next to her—whoever "her" is. For instance, you meet a woman at a party, and you see her look you up and down—she takes in everything head to toe and then she measures it—and herself. If she still feels good about herself, then you're okay. If she feels insecure, then it could get sticky. Really, then, a number of things could happen, running the gamut from you being sabotaged to her trying to be your best friend, perhaps in accordance with the philosophy of "keeping your friends close and your enemies closer."

Then there are the friends who have to one-up everything you do. If you mention a new restaurant you'd like to try, they make a reservation and go there first. If you get a membership at the country club, they do too. I think it's called "keeping up with the Joneses." But that's not really the type of jealousy I struggle with. I have never really been jealous of my friends' material possessions. The jealousy I struggle with occurs in my relationships with men. I have always lived with this fear that my boyfriend, or later, husband, was going to cheat. I don't know why I feel this way. My parents have been married more than thirty years. And my father has never been anything but committed and faithful to my mother. And yet I am tortured by the idea that I will be the victim of relational unfaithfulness. I even worry about my friends. I actually told one friend that if she married her boyfriend he unequivocally would cheat on her. And I truly believed it.

64

Every romantic relationship I've been in has been riddled with my jealousy and insecurity. If I suspected my significant other of even looking at another woman I would challenge him. And now that I'm married, I do the same thing. I am thoroughly convinced that my husband will cheat. My husband and I moved because he got a job transfer to another branch of his company. It was a new state, a new city, a new office. When I dropped him off at work one day, I sat in the parking lot for a few minutes after he disappeared inside. I observed the other employees arriving for work. And I began to think, *This is where it will happen. This is where my husband will cheat on me.* I wondered which of the women I had seen enter the building it would be.

The thing is, I'm a fairly confident woman in some respects. I know that I'm attractive to my spouse. I've given birth to two children, but I know I still look pretty good. I work out, eat right, and take care of my body. Sure, I don't think I'm necessarily beautiful, and sometimes I don't like what I see in the mirror, but the bottom line is this: I can still put on a pair of great-fitting black pants, zip on some high-heeled boots, and turn heads. And since unfortunately we all measure our value by the ability to turn heads, I know I still look pretty good. And I'm smart too—I'm educated and successful in my career. Those things help me to feel more confident about myself. But I still measure myself against every woman I see, and if I feel a particular woman is more attractive than me, then I am sure my husband will concur and it will all be over for me.

Since we've been married—and it's been nearly ten years—we've never been to a company party, either for his job or mine, that didn't end with a fight between us. We end up sleeping in separate rooms every time. And it is always for the same reason. I misread friendliness or harmless flirtation, sure that more is going on. Once my husband introduced me to a girl at work and told me later he wanted to set her up with one of his friends. I was immediately convinced that it was because he secretly wanted to be with her, and because he couldn't, well, then he wanted his friend to have her. Every time he tells me about a new girl at work, I ask him if she's attractive, I grill him on all her specs. If she is good looking, then I obsess over it. Every couple of months, he has to drive to a neighboring city to work out of another office location, and there is a woman in his office with whom he carpools. On those days, I'm a complete wreck. I fixate on it all day. I picture them in the car, hamming it up; she laughs at his jokes, and he feels pleased that he is a funny guy—and then they bond. If he should buy her a cup of coffee to repay her for buying gas, then I get neurotic. I actually look at his receipts when he comes home.

The thing is, he doesn't do anything to perpetuate my insecurity. Like my father was to my mother, he is only good and faithful to me. And anyway, I have him on such a tight leash he's afraid to talk to another woman. And still, I fear . . .

I know it's completely neurotic. I know! And yet there are more stories I could tell. Even when he's *with* me, I am afraid he'll want to look at another woman. On our honeymoon we vacationed in Mexico. One evening we enjoyed dinner at a quiet and romantic restaurant. It was small, with dim lighting and lots of intimate booths. I had bought a new outfit for every day of our honeymoon, and I was feeling pretty good in a cute and flirty little sundress. Our waitress came over to greet us and take our drink orders. Instantly I felt threatened by her. She was dark-skinned and exotic looking. The women from that culture are just more alluring and sultry—and she was definitely both of those things! I felt insecure with my overexposed white, creamy skin that had just left New England in February. And she laughed and flirted with him. And he laughed at her humor.

Didn't anyone tell her? Had she never learned how you should always make eye contact with the woman when talking to a couple so as to not make her feel threatened? Well, this woman apparently didn't know that unwritten rule—or didn't care. I looked down and glanced at my legs showing beneath my wispy dress. Their paleness practically blinded me. And then I saw her legs, tanned and long—of course. And I felt instantly desperate. This was my honeymoon. I was supposed to be the sexy, captivating wife. I had spent a fortune on clothes that could transform me into a sex goddess. It was a wardrobe I could never be seen in back home—sultry tops, strappy dresses, a sexy bikini, all just for him, and now I was sure he wanted to be with our waitress and not me. In desperation, when she left to get our drinks, promising, unfortunately, that she'd be back, I suggested we head to the bathroom for a quickie. Even as I said it I couldn't believe myself. I'm sure I hoped he wouldn't take me up on it. And he didn't. He thought I was crazy, and he laughed, disregarding the idea. He assumed I couldn't possibly be serious. And therein lies the problem—or at least one of them. I behave so insecurely that I compromise who I really am. I do things that are completely unnatural and not me. I was suggesting sex with my husband, in a dirty, smelly public restroom, to compete with a total stranger!

But my feelings of jealousy control me. They hold me back, and I spend hours fixated on every possible scenario, sure that I'll be left, abandoned and feeling ugly. Even now, as I sit at a crossroads where I must choose to have another child or move further in my career, I think I may choose the career in case I need the backup. What if I should have to support myself and my children?

I know my behavior is crazy, but it's primal and instinctual and I don't know how to tame it. I read the Bible, and it says that love is not jealous. And yet I am. And if I'm honest I think my jealousy is actually sin. And I get so frustrated because I keep doing the same sins over and over no matter how hard I try not to. I am still jealous, I still talk bad about people, even stab them in the back, I have negative thoughts even though I try so hard to stop those things. I pray, I meditate, I try harder. Will I always have these patterns? Will I have the same sins ten years from now?

I once read an article about Carolyn Bessette Kennedy in *Vanity Fair* magazine. It talked about when Carolyn and John were dating. Carolyn could work a room and did, when they went to parties together. She flirted shamelessly with the men, tossing her long blond hair, enrapturing them. Carolyn, of course, was beautiful. And John Kennedy was jealous. In an effort to get back at her, he too began to flirt with the other women in the room. But Carolyn didn't care. She was untouchable. Her attitude screamed, "Take it or leave it, I don't care." She was that confident—at least so the article said. When I read the article I found myself wishing that I could be that confident. I wished that I just didn't care. But I do care.

Sometimes I think it would take something really terrible to enable me to conquer this jealousy within me. Something like my husband actually having an affair and leaving me. Then I would have to make it on my own; I would have to raise my children alone. I'd get really strong, and then I'd be able to be like Carolyn and say, "Take it or leave it, boys." I'd become rock solid; I wouldn't have that dependence on another person. I don't really want that, of course. I don't want tragedy to make me strong. So there has to be something else.

In spite of everything, I am happy to say, though, that over time I have actually gotten less neurotic. As I've aged, I've grown, and as I look back I see how events in my life have given me that strength, however small. And so perhaps I can gain strength in experience by surviving the smaller things. And perhaps those lightweight events will culminate into a force to be reckoned with. Kind of like men benching at the gym. They pile on weight after weight to a single bar, starting with the larger, heavier disks, then adding smaller ones before securing them. Then they lie down on the bench under that enormous weight and proceed to lift it up, red-faced, veins in their necks bulging. I can lift the bar with no weight on it, and I can lift each individual weight that is slid onto the rod, but when it's all put together, I couldn't budge that weight an inch. I'm just not strong enough. But I could work up to it; over time I could gain in strength and success.

When I gave birth to my first child, a daughter, I felt inadequate. I didn't know what on earth to do with this baby, this little helpless person, and yet I gained a confidence in being a mother I never expected. It was hard to figure out breastfeeding, or how to change a diaper in a restaurant bathroom without a changing table. What was I to do with the baby day after day as I left my job to stay home with her full-time? But I figured it out. I survived, and I grew as a person. I matured. And not only that, now there are two little people who think the world revolves around me. I am their whole world, at least for a time. They cry for me. They think I can solve their problems. And the thing is, I can—for now. I can wipe those tears, I can make them smile, I can make them happy, and I can make everything okay. That's some potent power!

So why can't I see myself even just a little through their eyes? Why can't I believe that I have value—lasting value, not just an ability to be more beautiful and sexy than another woman? And why can't I find peace not only in my successes as they come but also in my relationship with my God, who loves me and who has said he would never leave me?

Discussion Questions

1. What makes you feel secure? What makes you feel insecure?
2. What do you find yourself being jealous or envious of?
3. What do you think it would take for you not to feel jealous?
4. Do you think men struggle with jealousy the way women do?

5

depleting myself for the sake of others

*Inside myself is a place where I live all alone
and that's where you renew your springs that
never dry up.*

—Pearl Buck

HAVE TO ADMIT, it's hard for me to be vulnerable with people, to be honest about my fears, my flaws, my failures. I mean, I want to be real, I want to be transparent. And I know the good that can come from it. But every time I am open, I get burned. I look at other people who are open and real, and I envy them.

73

I envy them because I want to be like that, and yet I am afraid to. And I envy them because somewhere in my mind I think it's easier for them than it is for me. My husband is the head of a prominent ministry in the small town we live in, and it's like living in a glass house. People peer in at us all the time—they may affirm or judge, and they most always talk.

There are times when someone will say something about my personal life to me, and I want to scream at them, "How in the heck did you find that out?" But I never do. What good would it do? It's like trying to plug one hole in a watering can. There are still fifty other holes from which the water can escape. So instead I close myself up and make myself crazy worrying about what people are saying about me and who else they're telling. I hate the thought that I may be dinner table conversation. And it's not that I'm being narcissistic; I'm speaking from experience.

People have such high expectations for me and my family. They look to us for guidance, for advice, and for wisdom. And if we do anything to disappoint them, they let us know. I feel like they expect me to be perfect. If I'm not available when they want me to be, or if I make a mistake, if I sin as we all do, then I am judged even more harshly. We sit atop a pedestal that I never wanted to be on, don't feel qualified to sit on. And if I thought I could jump off of it, I would. But for now, I can't. I can't because my husband and I are called to this ministry—at least for right now.

And so I hold things inside; I don't share who I really am. And I try not to need people to be there for me. I try to be there for them, and I receive love by taking care of other people. It all started when I was a child. I learned how to earn love, and I shut down and never cried. I thought not crying meant I couldn't be vulnerable. I was a cheerleader in high school, volunteered with the downtown food bank, I made really good grades, and I was prom queen. In college I was president of my sorority and was always giving, giving, giving. My mother often remarks to me and to others that my husband and I are the "pillars" of our family. When the family is in a crisis, I am the one who is always there. I've been there for car accidents, sicknesses, moving days, births, birthdays, and every holiday. They depend on me, and I rise to the occasion every single time. For a very long time, I've just been large and in charge. And so I'd go out and save the world, then return home, my superhero cape dragging behind me, and retreat to my bedroom, close the blinds, and have nothing left to give. I was empty. I am empty.

The truth is I am so very lonely. I am lonely because I so desperately want someone to take care of me. If I were to jump off that pedestal, or even just fall, I want someone to catch me, but there is no one. Even when I have struggled with depression, my mother's response has been the exasperated advice: "Quit feeling sorry for yourself and go help someone else." And I do. I always do. I have picked myself up and gone back out there, back into the trenches so to speak, feeling empty and yet looking for every opportunity to help others, and hoping that somewhere along the way I'd help myself at the same time.

I am an extremely sensitive person. I empathize and so desperately want to help people, but now I am so dry, so depleted. I just don't want to know anymore about people who are hurting and needy. And yet helping is what I do. It's my identity, it's my sense of self-worth, it's even my hiding place. It would disappoint everyone if I stopped.

And this desert within me is really no one's fault but my own. I am the one who gave myself away. I didn't care for myself, for my heart, my body, and my spirit. And when you don't care for yourself, you run out of things to give. It's not selfish to care for yourself, though women often tell themselves it is—or worse and more effectively, are told by others. It's holy. Yes, I believe it's holy to take care of what God has entrusted to you. And that includes your body inside and out, both physically and emotionally. Even Jesus took time to get away from the crowds; he rested, prayed, meditated, and was solitary and still at times. How can you use the gifts God has given you if you don't care for the vessel that possesses those very gifts? It's like not being able to drink water because there is no container from which to pour it. I have learned this the hard way, because at forty-eight I now see my body reacting to the years of intentional abandonment, not only physically but within my soul. I am reaping the manifestation of that neglect.

For years I battled depression off and on. My body is tight and tense with contained feeling. A massage therapist once commented to me after a massage that my body was holding something deep within. I knew she was right, but I kept it inside nonetheless. I have suffered with endometriosis that resulted in infertility. I tried for years to conceive but was unable, so we have not been able to have children. This has only further broken my heart. I couldn't imagine why God would do that to me. I felt as though I was doing every-thing for God, and he was doing nothing for me. Oh sure, I knew he did other things for me, but having children was the deepest longing of my heart. Yet, I can't help feeling that those problems are my body reacting to the feelings that I have locked up inside of me. It's like the negative emotion, not permitted to escape, has festered within me. Like a two-year-old wanting attention so badly even negative attention will do, my body is screaming out to me to pay it some mind. And I am starting to listen.

I wonder if the confined emotion attacked with intent the heart of my femininity. Endometriosis happens when the en-dometrial cells that should be contained in the uterus spread to other parts of the pelvic region. At best, it causes discomfort or cramping. At worst, and in my case, it causes infertility. I believe our uteruses, our ovaries, our breasts, the parts of our bodies that are unique to women, are what are most often attacked by stress and illness. It is only our gender, of course, that can give new life to another being. I wonder if it is our bodies getting back at us for the things we put them through—the neglect, the stress, the constant giving of energy without spending time to replace it.

And then I felt like my hair was thinning. And when stress attacked my thick head of hair—my hair that only now in my late forties is starting to gray—I got scared. I know it sounds shallow, but it moved me to action. I couldn't do anything about the endometriosis or the fact that I couldn't have children, but I could stop my hair from falling out. And I knew I needed to get control of my body, and to do that I needed to come to grips with all that was waging within me.

I have just begun my journey. And I first began it by allowing myself to cry. It says in Psalm 56 that God records our tears. God cares about every tear that falls. Perhaps he even knows the number. And it had been so long since I'd permitted any to fall. Now I can't stop. I cry so quickly, so easily. I realize I was trying to earn love and believing I wasn't lovable if I wasn't helping people. But that was a lie I had told myself or allowed myself to accept as truth.

And it's a process taking those lies captive. When I'm not pleasing people or being the perfect Christian woman, I beat myself up. I worry what people say behind my back, and I continue to give of myself over and over as if by always doing something for someone, I will make them love me. And it's not true, but it so often feels true, you know?

I'm in my late forties, but I am just now realizing the way my mind works. I think the only way to not believe the lies is to put truth in place of the lies. What does God believe about me? Am I trying to earn his love too? I have believed in God and have had a personal relationship with him for a long time. But not until recently have I been able to say that I really love God. I love and need him. He is showing me much that is on my heart, and I am learning to lean. I started to take walks to talk to God. When I am out in nature, I feel his presence the most. I need to clear my head and get away from all the distractions around me. I need to escape from all the things I do to fill the space. When I need to know what to do I go away for a time and try to listen. I need to be still before God. People who are wise are often silent; they speak from that quietness or they speak from pain. There is a depth to their wisdom that you can't see but you know is there. I have begged before, I have pleaded in the past, and I have reasoned, but then there is my time to be silent.

But I realized something too. If I don't spend time with God on a regular basis, then when I need to hear his voice I don't hear anything. I don't know that it's because he isn't speaking to me, but perhaps it is because I don't recognize the sound of his voice. And I need to hear his voice. In order to learn how to give of myself in a way that is healthy, I need to know and hear from God. God isn't just available on demand. You need to have a relationship. At least that is what I have learned. And I've learned to know when he is speaking to me. Perhaps so often I know because it's exactly the opposite of what I would have chosen to do or what I think God would have me do. I am still on this journey; I don't know what things will be ahead, what pain, or what triumph. All I know is that right now there is God and there is me. And I suppose that will be enough.

Discussion Questions

1. Do you think you're real with others?
2. How does the statement "you have to take care of yourself before you can take care of others" make you feel?
3. Do you think you try to earn love?

6

needing to be beautiful

HEATHER

In the faces of men and women I see God.

—Walt Whitman

I USED TO WATCH the show *Extreme Makeover* every Sunday night. It came on a little later than I preferred, and often I planned to watch for a little while then head off to bed. But I always stayed until the very end. Once I saw how unattractive the people selected were to begin with, I just had to find out how it all turned out. First, they leave their families for several weeks. Then they see a cosmetic surgeon who consults with them on all the surgeries that are recommended. They begin to look like a road map after the doctor draws with a marker on the areas on which to have surgery. Liposuction on the thighs, a nose job, a chin implant, breast implants, a tummy tuck—all are sketched on this human guinea pig. After they have begun to recover from their surgeries they may visit a dentist for caps or veneers and an eye doctor for LASIK surgery so that the eyeglasses can be discarded. Then there is a hairstylist and colorist, a wardrobe consultant, a makeup artist, a nutritionist and personal trainer. All this so they can feel like a whole new person, and most importantly beautiful. After much anticipation, at the very end of the show they finally allow you, the viewer, to see what all the surgery, dieting, and stylist consultations produced. And it is the moment when their friends and family finally see them too. At their grand unveiling they are greeted by shock, cheering, and ebullient excitement, even tears of joy.

Week after week I watched men and women who have felt hindered by their physical appearance their entire lives. As I listened to them tell story after story of rejection usually beginning from childhood, but continuing even as adults, I hurt for them. And to see their tears of happiness at their new appearance is so heartrending. A beautiful appearance was their dream come true, and probably a dream they never even dared hoped for, and for right or wrong I think they thought most of their problems would be solved now. I have always wondered if at that moment of revelation in front of the world they thought they were a better person, or had more to contribute to the world now that they were beautiful. And I wonder, *Are they disappointed when they go back home and their lives return to normal?*

It seems so "extreme," and it is, of course. That's partly the fascination, why I and thousands of other people watched the show. Most people could never pay for all those surgeries. But then I think of my getting-ready routine and all the effort I put into my appearance each day. After showering with a moisturizing liquid soap—because I read in a beauty book that you should never use bar soap on your body—I carefully pat my skin dry. I slather lotion on my body; the lotion has a little shine in it to make my skin glow. Then I turn my attention to my face, and after washing it with expensive face cleanser, I swipe an eye cream around my eyes in a figure eight motion, then I moisturize the rest of my face with a different cream and make sure to hit my neck with it as well. And I smooth on sunblock.

Then there's makeup. I cover any blemishes on my face, use another moisturizer, now a tinted one, sweep on eye shadow to enhance my eye color, put blush on the apples of my cheeks to give me a fresh, flushed appearance. Mascara makes my eyelashes look longer and thicker, and I finish off with lipstick, dabbing a bit of clear gloss on top of the lip color in the dip of my lip to make my lips look fuller.

I do all this to create the look that my culture says is beautiful. My routine and the products I use are put together by beauty magazines that I read voraciously. And there are studies done to tell us what is considered beautiful. For example, contrast with the eyes and lips, or lips and skin has always created a perception of beauty. So a woman with dark hair, milky skin, and red lipstick would turn heads of both men and women. Or the proportion of your face, the distance between your eyes, and the relative symmetry between all the facial features are tried-and-true measurements that qualify as true beauty. And then there are the surveys in magazines like *Cosmo* or *Glamour* that ask men about what body parts they prefer. I don't know why it's helpful for me to know that Derek, 24, in Seattle likes legs, but we chase this information, read this stuff, and determine how attractive we are accordingly. And it's shallow, indeed, even degrading. Who is Derek to judge me?

But it's true, you know, for both men and women, that their physical appearance often determines their success. An attractive child is often favored by the teacher from the time he or she enters school. Strangers are nice to them, and they have friends from a very young age. This establishes a confidence within them that empowers many of the choices they make along the way, giving them a higher chance for success. Even as adults, they are more likely to land jobs, make more sales, and move higher within the company. It is sad, but I think it's true. People think that if you're not beautiful then you have to have something else going for you—either brains or humor.

Thankfully there are a variety of looks, features, and combinations that we find beautiful. There is tall and leggy, petite and delicate, blond and blue eyed, dark hair and brown eyed, tanned glowing skin, or creamy alabaster. And there are different things we find beautiful on the person we love—a gesture, a fluttered eyelash, a laugh.

Beauty in the world around us is important to us too. We spend time and money building beautiful homes, cultivating exquisite gardens, setting an appealing table for a dinner party. We walk on the beach, hike in the fall to enjoy the leaves, take pictures of sunsets and flowers. We want to be surrounded by beauty, and we spend a great deal of energy creating it.

Sometimes I think to myself, *AIDS is wiping out entire villages in Africa. Why do I care that Lancôme just came out with a new long-wearing lipstick?* But the truth is, beauty matters the world over, even in Africa.

I'm a faithful fan of Oprah. I TiVo her show every single day, and I own the DVD collection. She did a story one day about young women and girls in a particular area of Africa. The girls were giving birth at such a young age that when they were pushing to deliver their babies they were ripping their bladders. After childbirth, the tears in their bladders remained open and then leaked. It made the girls unclean—they smelled, no one wanted to be around them, and they were isolated in their villages, rejected and ostracized. Finally, a woman, a doctor, went into the villages and began performing surgeries on the girls so that they could return to living a normal life. After an appropriate recovery time, they were allowed to go back to their villages. And back to their lives. Imagine how they must feel. After being outcasts, they were able to live normal lives again. They felt like new people.

Before returning to their villages, the women asked for one thing. They wanted a pretty dress to wear to return home in. Their lives were changed, their bodies healed, but they still wanted to feel pretty. Probably feeling so filthy and undesirable had made them feel ugly, and now they desired the feeling of beauty again. I sat watching the TV with tears rolling down my face. I identified so much with those women. They were far away from me in so many aspects, geographically, experientially, yet I felt connected to them, connected by our desire to be beautiful.

Yes, there are different interpretations of beauty, but we all desire to be beautiful just the same. I think you are lying if you say you don't. Even a woman like Gail Evans has that desire to be beautiful. Gail Evans is a woman who has enjoyed a very successful career. Beginning her career in the office of special counsel for the Lyndon B. Johnson administration, she later ascended the ranks at CNN to become the first female senior executive vice president. Gail has also written two books; her first, *Play Like a Man, Win Like a Woman*, was translated into multiple languages and was a bestseller around the world. She has her own syndicated weekly radio segment and is a visiting professor at Georgia State University. In the book *Midlife Crisis at Thirty* by Lia Macko and Kerry Rubin, Gail opens up to readers about her greatest risk. She tells the world that her greatest risk was standing up in front of people, first in meetings and later on television and in classrooms. Was she afraid of public speaking? Not exactly. Her greatest risk was standing up before audiences and not being beautiful. When

I read those words, I literally had to stop reading, sit back, and take it in. Gail went on to say that not being beautiful was the most difficult thing for her. I just couldn't believe it. Here was an incredibly smart, talented, and successful woman who worked her way up a corporate ladder of "good ole boys." And she felt insecure because she didn't think she was beautiful.

The desire for beauty is the essence of my soul. For me it is consuming. Because I not only desire to be beautiful but I also need to be the most beautiful. Being merely pretty isn't enough. I need to feel that I am everything for the man I am with, and I think that is found in being the fairest of them all.

I think the evil queen in *Snow White* is misunderstood. Granted, she took things a bit too far when she tried to kill her stepdaughter. But even in a children's fairy tale the desire for beauty is palpable. As a little girl I longed to be beautiful. I used to watch the every move of a woman that I thought was pretty. To me, it was as if a beautiful woman was the magical Snow White herself. And though I don't stand in front of my mirror talking to it every day, I stand before it hoping that I will be the most beautiful. The thing is, I never think I am, and so I live in fear of being rejected for not being pretty enough. In any social situation, I do this thing: I case the room. You know what I mean. I walk into the room and immediately size up the other women in it. I take in each woman's height, clothes, accessories, shoes, hair, and figure. If she has a great figure but made a bad shoe choice, I feel a little better. If her outfit is cute but she's a little overweight, again I breathe a sigh of relief. If I am

87

not the most beautiful woman in the room, then I want to leave. If a woman is thin but has large breasts, I'm sure my husband will wish he could be with her. Or if she is tall and thin, model-like, I feel short and round in comparison. The thing is, if my husband were having a stimulating conversation with another woman, I wouldn't be threatened. But if she is more beautiful, then I am crushed. I fear losing his attention.

From the time I started dating I feared not being the most beautiful. I remember hearing boys talk about girls over lunch in the cafeteria. They compared us against each other, and all the boys seemed to be looking for the perfectly beautiful girl. If a girl was pretty but had a few less-than-perfect features, they pointed it out. Many of the boys I dated would be critical of me, always suggesting something to improve, either implants, working out, or weight loss. I got the message that looks were important, so important that it was the only way to hold my boyfriends, and now my husband.

The reflection in his eyes is the one I see, and if I am the most beautiful, then I have the most value, and I am okay. I do know now that there is more to who I am. That is to say, I know this in my head. But to actually feel it, to live it is another matter. When I consider my value as a woman, I know that Jesus held women in very high esteem and not because of their physical beauty. And I know that it is the reflection in his eyes that matters the most. But of course it takes much more work to see the eyes of God. And often this sounds like spiritual answers that are easy to say but so much harder to really live. Especially when those answers are overshadowed every day by a barrage of messages all around me that say beauty is what matters.

But what would it take for me to accept my body and in turn my whole self? What would it take for me to be able to look at my body and know it's not perfect but love it anyway? What would it require for me to start with my feet and say: I love my feet because they help me to stand, my ten toes give me balance, without them I'd have to sit or crawl. And I can buy really cool shoes to wear on them. I love my legs because they make me feel strong, they support the weight of my body, and, even more, they take me places. I can walk, I can run, I can go wherever I want to go because I have my two legs. I love my abdomen because even though it's softer than I want on the outside, inside it is life giving. Beneath that fleshy exterior I can give life to another human being, something that only a woman can do. I love my breasts because though they are smaller than I would like them to be they are mine. And they are part of what makes me feel feminine. I love my neck because it turns my head. I couldn't see everything I want to see without my neck. I couldn't look up and see a full, white moon or a zillion stars. With my mouth, I can speak, I can eat, I can smile, and I can kiss. My ears hear music and waves crashing, and the voice of those I love telling me they love me too. My nose can smell homemade spaghetti cooking, brownies fresh from the oven, springtime air, and when snow is on its way. My eyes can see all the beauty of the world around me. They see the ugliness too, but that is what gives me perspective and makes me appreciate the beauty. That is me. That is my physical body filled with imperfections, but it still enables my fullness of life.

I think if I were to be sick, or need a mastectomy because of breast cancer, or lose my hearing, or have a leg amputated, how much I would miss that part of my body! And then it would be too late to appreciate it. So why can't I appreciate it now? If I think to my future, at best my skin will be wrinkled, my breasts will sag, my lips will be even thinner, and my belly will be even rounder. But, worse, I may not have the gift of health I have now, and I will have wasted all these years competing with other women, sizing up my body parts and assets against theirs, and for what? What do I gain?

Even though I know all this to be true, why do I diminish my value as a human being, and as a woman? And yet I do, I admit it, I do. And I don't know how to feel differently about myself and about being beautiful. I know how to think, or how I should think, but to feel is much harder.

A group of women were meeting together for a Bible study every week. This was a group of women with rough and sordid backgrounds. Many had been abused and used, been in jail, had drug addictions, and many had been literally rescued off the street. They met together every week at a downtown church in New York City and were working through a study by Beth Moore. They hung on every truth spoken by this kind, well-spoken, Southern lady. One week the discussion turned to the innate desire of women to be beautiful. The talk volleyed around the circle as the women opened up and shared their deep desires of beauty. One woman finally piped up, "Yeah, I always wanted to be beautiful too. I used to pray that God would just make me beautiful. And then he did. I realized it one day when I was at my ex-husband's house. He had a picture in a frame sitting on a bookcase. And I thought to myself, *Who's that good-looking woman he's with?*" She paused for a second and continued on. "I leaned in closer and saw it was me! *Girl, you're one good-looking woman,* I told myself! He's a lucky man to have been married to a woman as beautiful as me.

"So I knew God had answered my prayer," she finished.

It seemed that God had literally changed the eyes with which she looked at herself. Did she see herself through God's eyes? Is that what it would be like? Because it wouldn't have mattered if anyone had told her that she wasn't actually beautiful. She knew she was, and that was all that mattered. I wish so much I had her confidence—and her eyesight. She didn't say that God changed her desire to be beautiful. She said that he actually made her beautiful! And I got to thinking that God wouldn't change our desire for beauty; I think that's a part of who we are, and we are a people created to appreciate what is beautiful. Why else would God create so much beauty around us? But the importance we place on beauty—that can change. I know I want it to change in me. But I guess it's a process and a work that is done over time. And it would seem that even the way we see ourselves can change too. I want that vision!

Discussion Questions

1. How do you define beauty?
2. Why do you think it is important to women to feel beautiful?
3. Do you think it is possible for you to come to a place where beauty doesn't matter? What would have to happen to bring that about?
4. Is beauty more important to women than it is to men?

7

willingness

FAITH

You desire to know the art of living, my friend?
It is contained in one phrase: make use of
suffering.

—Henri-Frédéric Amiel

'M NOT AFRAID to look deep into my own soul. Yes, it's scary and doing so is often messy, but I can look at it nonetheless. It wasn't always this way; until a few years ago, I never looked deep within myself. I didn't think about how the things that went on around me applied to me, affected me, or had any significance to me. I just wasn't willing to really examine myself and my soul, looking directly at what I saw, thought, and did. And if I ever caught a glimpse of something inside me that I might not like, I certainly never shared it with others. I was too afraid of the look I'd see in their eyes, looks of judgment, of rejection, and of not loving me anymore. So instead I emptied myself over and over. I gave myself away to others, giving up my own opinions, my ideas, and my own will.

I did this in part because I care immensely about the people in my life. Relationships are so important to me that I poured everything into them. As a result I have many friends; I even keep in touch with people from college, even though it's been many years since I graduated. People always came to me for help and friendship because they knew they could count on me, and I always responded with my whole heart.

And then tragedy came into the lives of several of my friends at the same time. One of my dearest friends got breast cancer. She was married and had young children, and she fought her illness with all she had, both for herself and for them, but she lost her battle. I carried the pain of her disease inside of me while she lived. I brought meals for her family, I went with her to chemo treatments, I helped her in any way I could. And when she died, her death cast a shadow over my heart. I needed to grieve deeply, but I didn't have the chance. I didn't take the chance. The grief was too messy, and I wasn't ready to go there yet. Immediately after her death, my neighbors lost their child when he drowned in the swimming pool. I was the first one to arrive at the scene. I found the child, then had to explain everything to the police. I had to tell the parents, who were my friends, and repeat the story for others over and over. And I just gave of myself entirely. I felt as though I was surrounded by so much pain and I needed to let it go; only, once again, I ignored that need. It wasn't until six months later that I first gave a thought to myself and how the deaths affected me. But when I'd let myself think deeply, I saw haunting images or memories that threatened me. So I brushed them away; again, it seemed messy, even dark and ugly.

Some people consciously don't think of themselves, actively deciding to be what they deem as unselfish. Others know they are neglecting themselves but draw comfort in being a martyr or they think the depths of grief, the messiness of raw emotion, is unchristian. After all, what about the saying that has become cliché: "it's not about you." I felt things, but when I empathized with a friend, it was just about her. I never gave a thought to any insight or implication for myself. Did any of the tragedy around me affect me personally, or was it only happening to others?

Eventually I began to feel so heavy from the weight of carrying other people's problems. I allowed them to be sewn like fabric into my soul, and I felt as though a rock had lodged itself into my heart.

I felt like Sue Monk Kidd's character, tenderhearted May, in *The Secret Life of Bees*. May is a large black woman living in South Carolina in 1964. And she has a deeply tender soul. She feels for others so deeply that it cripples her. When she hears of any pain or mishap, anything from rotten vegetables to a stillborn baby, she has what you might call a "spell," her empathy is so deep. August and June, her two sisters, do everything they can to help her. They build what they call a "wailing wall" in the back of their house. Built of stones held together by a little cement, the wall is knee high and stretches almost fifty yards. When May becomes overcome by heartache, she writes about it on paper and sticks the paper into the crevices created by the stacked stones. After one tragic event, even the wailing wall does nothing to assuage her grief. June and August give May a bath to settle her down, hoping the water running over her will wash away the pain. But May eventually is so overcome by the pain of others that she wades into the river one dark night, and with each person's heartache like stones in her pocket, she goes below the surface of the water and never emerges.

I, like May, was beginning to wade into some dark waters as a result of too much pain. I convinced myself that I was going to die. I was sure of it, and it petrified me. Sure, people say that when you're a Christian you shouldn't be afraid to die, but I was overcome. I had small children that were going to lose their mother. I know it doesn't make sense, but I was sure that God was going to take me off this earth before I had completed what he wanted me to do. Much of the time our fears are irrational, but they are lodged so deep within our hearts that even a scolding from our heads doesn't frighten them away. And so I lived with this crippling fear of dying, and I was determined to outsmart death if only by knowing it was coming and so not giving it the benefit of surprise. So where once I never applied other people's tragedies to myself, I now took every illness in another person and looked for truth for myself in it. I even imagined that God thought he was doing me a favor showing me that my death was coming.

One night before falling asleep I began to feel a tingling in my legs. I looked over at my sleeping husband beside me and wondered if I should wake him. I decided I didn't want to worry him. At first I thought, *It's diabetes, yes, I'm a diabetic. Well, that's okay. I can control it with diet, and even if you have to take insulin, diabetics can live a full and long life. They are making huge strides in the medical field with diabetes. Maybe one day I can even be cured. I can still see my children graduate from high school and college, even get married.* But then a thought made its way to my already panicked mind. *What if it's MS? Still, that doesn't mean I'll die. Maybe I'll be in a wheelchair. I know that'll be hard for my kids, but they would still love me, wouldn't they? There may be a way to keep it under control. What are my options—surgery, medication?* I promised myself I would research MS in the morning as soon as my husband was off to work and my children had left for school. And with that promise I finally fell asleep.

In the morning, once alone, I went to my computer. I googled "leg twitching," and as I waited for the results, I felt my heart pounding. I sifted through the results and was starting to click on a link for multiple sclerosis when I saw another link below—ALS—also known as Lou Gehrig's disease. I felt my stomach flip three times and land with a thud in my gut. My mind flashed to a novel I'd read a couple years ago. The book was called *The First Time*, and it was about a woman who had ALS. The memories of all she went through poured over my mind.

I was panicked and certain that I had diagnosed myself. I went to my family doctor but didn't tell him what I thought I had; he didn't seem to think anything was wrong. So then I made an appointment to see my gynecologist. While sitting in the waiting room, I glanced at the coffee table, intending to pick up a magazine to read while passing the time. I noticed a *People* magazine, and on the front cover was a headline for a story Katie Couric had done on Lou Gehrig's disease. I looked at the magazine, wanting so much to pick it up. A voice inside me told me to leave it. But I wondered if it was a sign, something telling me that I did indeed have ALS. But then the receptionist called my name, and as it turned out there was something wrong with my insurance card and they wouldn't accept it. So I had to make another appointment for a week later.

When I went back the following week, the magazine was still lying on the coffee table. Now I knew it was a sign, and I picked it up and read through it quickly before being called in by the nurse. And as I read about the way the ALS patients described the way the disease felt at the onset, I became convinced that I had the disease. I practically trembled. When I went in to see the doctor I told her about the leg twitches, and she said she didn't know what that would be, then moved on to something else. She wasn't the expert I needed, though. I knew, from the novel I'd read, that I needed to go to a neurologist.

Even though I was so sure I had the disease, I was too afraid to have the diagnosis confirmed. I know, it makes no sense, but I was gripped by terror, and I guess there was a part of me that thought I could be wrong. But if the doctor confirmed my self-diagnosis, well, then death was imminent. My life was all but flashing before my eyes.

My friends tried to convince me I was fine, or to at least see a doctor to put my mind at ease. They kept telling me that I was experiencing signs of anxiety and not Lou Gehrig's. But I was sure they were wrong and sure that God was telling me so. First, I had that feeling that I was going to die, then I felt the twitches, then I accidentally found the info on ALS on the Internet, then I saw the magazine article. I was sure God had led me to these conclusions in a warped scavenger hunt. I went online again to do more research. I looked up the symptoms for anxiety: I had all of them. I looked up the symptoms for ALS: I had maybe two, and it was a vague match at best. But still, ALS won over in my mind.

After pressure from my friends and pleading from my husband, I agreed to go to see a doctor, this time a neurologist. This was a huge step for me. The truth is it was a spiritual step because by going to the doctor, I was believing that God was greater than my fear. In essence I was saying to God, "Okay, I have ALS, but you will be there for me. Whatever I have to go through after the diagnosis, I am trusting you." And then I said, "If it's my time, then fine, but I am not offering my body up to the devil on a silver platter." I don't know where that even came from; I had never really thought about spiritual warfare stuff before. But it was a resolve that emerged from somewhere inside me. And then off I went to the neurologist to face my fate.

I didn't have ALS. I actually had severe anxiety. All that time of leaving feelings unexamined and not acknowledging the stress caused by all I had experienced was more than my body could handle, and it was trying to tell me something. And I was just hearing the wrong thing.

Speaking of hearing, I not only learned I wasn't going to die—at least not yet—I learned so much about hearing from God. Probably many people can't relate to what they would see as my irrational fear, but we all have fears, and maybe to others they seem silly. But mine have taught me more than I could have imagined. To begin with, my fears forced a willingness in me to look at my heart, my sin, my control, my mistrust, and it was messy, just as I secretly feared. But as I grew in faith and in knowledge of myself, I learned more about my body and experienced more of God. I became better able to hear what God says to me. As I read my Bible and spend time in prayer with God, and as I have learned to pay attention to what happens within me, I sense inside my heart that God is speaking, and I also see this confirmed in other ways. And not neurotic ways! I have learned how to recognize what I know and what God reveals to me personally. It's twofold, trusting yourself just enough and trusting God. But I don't think it's about a practical to-do list to arrive at that place of trust. And it is willingness to go to those places we fear. I only discovered it through experience—I know my experiences, I know myself, and I know my soul, and I have trusted even when I didn't know the ending. It is knowledge, it is intuition, it is experience.

Discussion Questions

1. How honest do you think you are about yourself, with yourself?
2. Do you think there is anything about who you are that you are not consciously aware of?
3. What things in your life prevent you from taking an honest look at your own heart?

8

whom do I serve?

MARY JANE

It is never too late to be what you might have been.

—George Eliot

THINK ONE OF the strengths that women share is the ability to multitask. A woman can take a phone call while making dinner with a baby on her hip, all the while needing to be somewhere in twenty minutes. Whether we feel like it or not, we are most often up to the task of multitasking.

But I think because we have this talent for juggling, we take on too much. For me, that is certainly true. I have spent much of my adult life attending church functions, making casseroles for sick friends, throwing showers for friends, taking care of the neighbors' children. And I expected to do it all with flair and perfection. But if I'm truthful, I've done much of what I've done not simply because I'm a good multitasker but because of fear and the need to earn people's love.

Unfortunately, in my efforts to please other people, I neglected my own family. It's so much easier to serve others than to serve your own family. I thought my family would love me no matter what; or maybe I just got more affirmation from other people. The sick person from my church would tell me how wonderful I was even if she had to hoist herself up from bed to tell me so. And women appreciate what other women do. What we wear and how well our shoes match our outfits, how perfect our manicure is, how we decorate, the thoughtful extra kindnesses like cards, little gifts, and flowers do not go unnoticed by women, at least compared to a husband and children.

I grew up in a very affluent and nonreligious family, and my father was often too busy to give time to our family. He worked hard and was very successful and a wonderful provider. But he was absent too. When I was a teenager, though, he became a Christian. Impassioned by his new commitment, he quit his job and decided to go to seminary. We had to sell our house and move to a poor neighborhood. Used to having nice things, I was very embarrassed by our house. And fearful that people would no longer like me, I found other ways to earn affection and popularity; I invested myself in people. Which is a wonderful thing, but I lived to make people happy because I thought that would make them love me.

And so I stretched myself. I did everything in a big way for everyone. I bought the loveliest or most unique gifts, threw the best parties, and was there whenever anyone needed help. I thought if I went overboard on everything, people would think the world of me. And they would talk to each other about how creative I was, or how talented, thoughtful, and godly. Before I had my own children I was a private tutor for a very wealthy family. I used to rack my brain over the lessons, trying to make them as creative as possible. When we were learning about the Vikings, I deemed it Viking day. I made Jell-O for whale blubber, and we dressed like Vikings and acted like Vikings eating off the floor and drinking root beer from frosty mugs. I wanted the parents, my employers, to come home and see everything I had done and think I was the greatest teacher they'd ever had. I wanted them to tell me how wonderful and smart I was.

One time I wanted to give a birthday gift to a woman in my neighborhood. I wanted the gift to really stand out, to be one that she would always remember. So I baked a beautiful cake that was made to look like a wicker basket. I covered it with white icing and heaped the inside high with fresh, juicy red strawberries that spilled over the edges. I presented it to her, acting like it was no big deal, and of course she exclaimed how delightful my gift was. But years later I overheard her

105

talking about the cake to some other women and saying how beautiful it was, but she couldn't remember who made it for her. I felt foolish. That experience made me wonder why I felt so compelled to make people happy. I had to do everything in a big way, always over the top, but why? I spent so much time doing things for other people that I neglected my family—until I was rudely shaken.

I had been nagging my husband for a long time to be more involved in our church. I was frustrated with him because I felt that he wasn't being a spiritual leader. So I harassed him—effective, right? Well, finally he signed up to go on a mission trip to Guatemala. He was gone for two weeks, and when he came back he seemed like a new person. He was energetic, happy, and enthusiastic about our church again. I secretly patted myself on the back for my expert spiritual coaching and then didn't give it another thought. Now he was willing to go to church, whereas before he didn't seem to care that much. I noticed every time we went to church he was often talking to an attractive woman who had gone on the mission trip. It was nothing inappropriate, but he was always friendly with her. When it continued, and I noticed he always sought her out, I began to sense there was something more. I asked him about it, and he said that they had gotten to know each other on the trip. He agreed that they had bonded, but it still seemed innocent enough.

Still feeling a bit insecure, I joined a Bible study that she was in. I think I felt better if I kept an eye on her, though it was only a couple of hours once a week. But it seemed to make things worse. When I returned home he was full of questions, asking me about the study but most specifically what she had said about this and that. I realized this was not so innocent anymore. I confronted him about it, and we went to talk to our pastor. Nothing had happened between them, it was only friendship, but he admitted that he probably enjoyed the friendship more than he should. Actually it seemed to be one-sided, and she seemed to be oblivious that he had any attachment to her. I asked the pastor if we should leave the church. The pastor encouraged us to stay and was confident things would be okay; after all, no one had done anything wrong. A few weeks passed, and things seemed to be okay. My husband was being extra kind to me. I began to exhale a little, thinking the storm had passed. Then one day, when he got home from work he told me he had sent her a card.

Livid and humiliated, I got into my car and drove to the woman's house. I demanded she give the card to me. She seemed surprised by the whole thing. And honestly, I don't know why I did this. What purpose did it serve? I guess I was just feeling the life I'd created slipping out of my hands. I was angry, but also hurt.

I didn't know if I should stay with my husband. My hidden fears had come to pass. I was afraid he did not love me anymore because I had not done enough for him. I knew that I had been too busy. I had stopped investing in him, I had cared more about approval from other people, and I had lost his love. As much as we don't like to think of love as conditional, if you leave a heart uncared for, the love will eventually die. I just

107

didn't know what to do from there. But I decided I wanted to keep working on our marriage, and so did he. I went to God, telling him I desperately needed his help, and even saying, "You are not a woman, you can't understand how I feel."

In my struggles I thought of how Jesus wanted his disciples to stay and pray with him in the garden before his death. But they kept falling asleep. I realized that Jesus knew what it was like to be let down and even abandoned by those he trusted. I thought about the fact that I could never have died for those men when they couldn't even stay awake for me. I knew I could forgive my husband, even if it took a long time, because I was different now. I had always feared someone not loving me, not wanting me because I didn't do enough. But the thing is, I had done a lot of things, I just hadn't done them for the people closest to me.

Now it seemed what I feared had happened, and what was I going to do? I would survive. You think that emotional pain will kill you, that the worst thing you imagine will destroy you. It didn't kill me. I hate that saying "What doesn't kill you makes you stronger." I've never liked it because I hate clichés in the face of pain. But it was true, though painfully so.

It's not really about doing enough, anyway. I asked myself what I hoped in. I knew the Christian answer, of course: "My hope is in God." But it wasn't actually true. I'd been a Christian since I was a teenager, but I didn't even know how to hope in God. I hoped only in my other relationships and earning love and affirmation that would enable me to feel good about myself. But what a burden it was. A burden of trying to make other people love me. It was a never-ending task driving me to excess and perfection. And I sacrificed so much simply to look impressive in the eyes of others. But I needed to hope in God. I didn't exactly know how to start, to make it really literal and not just something I say. But I knew that God was the only one who would never stop loving me. I know it sounds so simple, but I don't mean it that way. It was quite profound for me.

I am forty-six years old and just realizing that my relationship with God is the only relationship that is immune to my worst fear. Recently I painted a picture. It's no spectacular masterpiece; its only purpose is to serve as a visual reminder for me. I hung it in my bathroom where I will see it every day. It's a picture of me on top of a rock. First I painted myself sitting on the rock, then lying on the rock, then jumping on the rock, finally standing on the rock. No matter how I change, what I do or don't do, the rock remains. I can't forget that truth.

Discussion Questions

1. What gives you a sense of self-worth?
2. What do you think has more value, doing or being? Does your life reflect this? If not, why?
3. Do you think it is possible to give of yourself too much?

9

courage

VICTORIA

*And so the hand of time will take the frag-
ments of our lives and make out of life's rem-
nants, as they fall, a thing of beauty, after all.*

—Douglas Malloch

MANY PEOPLE SAY they feel better after a good, hearty
cry. That gut-wrenching, intense crying over something bad is supposed to be healing. Perhaps it's our way of
expelling the bad that is inside in a physical way. It's sort of like

sweating. I remember my twelfth-grade physiology teacher telling me that sweating is our body's way of removing toxins.

So maybe those good, hard cries relieve our bodies of emotional toxins. With each tear that falls a bit of pain laced with disappointment or fury washes away. And even though after you have finished a good cry your face can look like someone punched you, your mascara may be collected in dark pools beneath your eyes, bits of tissue may be matted to your face, and you may have a splitting headache or be incredibly thirsty, there is some relief there too. And it's strange, because you can feel release even if nothing that first caused you to cry has changed.

But I didn't cry for decades. Actually, up until a year ago I couldn't remember when I last cried.

As a child I thought that there was a way to protect myself from being hurt. It was at least worth the attempt, I thought. I was a very sensitive little girl, and I had been hurt a lot even at a young age. I began to isolate myself from relationships. It was fairly easy because I was the only child of a blended family. This meant my siblings were all a good deal older than me. I spent a lot of time alone. I had friends in school, but I was very critical of them. I found that people always disappointed me, and I didn't like being disappointed. I found it difficult to accept others in their humanity. But I couldn't verbalize it to them or anyone else, so my disenchantment and their imperfection always became an impasse for me in the relationship. When people let me down I simply withdrew and let the relationship die a quiet death.

I tried other ways to shut out pain. I thought that not crying meant I wouldn't feel hurt. I heard a song on the radio once about not crying out loud, and I decided to make that my resolve. And so I stopped. I didn't cry when I was lonely, I didn't cry when I was disappointed, I didn't cry when I fell out of my tree house and broke my arm. I didn't cry when I didn't make cheerleading, I didn't cry when I broke up with my first boyfriend, and I didn't cry when my husband asked me to marry him. I didn't cry at my wedding—or anyone else's—I didn't cry when my three children were born. I saw *Beaches, Steel Magnolias,* and *An Affair to Remember,* I didn't shed one tear. I cared about many things, I cared very much, but I didn't cry. Eventually, I began to fear crying. I was afraid that if I ever did let myself cry, I wouldn't stop.

It's strange what brings you to the point of reckoning with yourself. So often it's not those moments that seem so profound, and yet they change you forever. My husband and I were trying to make a decision, and I knew what I wanted, and I wanted it desperately. My husband didn't agree. But I was always very good at getting what I wanted. I knew just how to manipulate to get my way without looking like I was getting my way. I would plant ideas and try to make them look like they were the ideas of the person I was trying to convince—usually my husband. I withheld information, I knew my husband's points of weakness, and I preyed on them, using them to convince him of what I wanted. I asked questions I already knew the answer to in an attempt to bring him to my conclusion. I used to hate it when my mother did that to me.

Asking questions in a way to get me to do what she wanted. She would manipulate me even with little things, like when she was at my house for dinner. She knew I was going to put the ketchup bottle on the table, which she thought was an eyesore. So before I had a chance to do so, she asked, innocently, if I was going to put the ketchup in a little dish.

I think we all manipulate to a degree, but I didn't like what I was seeing inside myself. My husband agreed to do what I wanted, though he qualified his agreement with the caution that he thought it was an unwise decision and that he was doing it to pacify me. And suddenly I began to see myself with greater awareness. I didn't like what I saw one bit. But at the same time I refused to shy away from it. Much of my refusing to cry was denial throughout my life, denying my weakness, my vulnerability. But here I was facing myself with audacity as if going toe to toe with my mirror image. And I knew that my experience, my reality, did not match up with the person I was, the person I knew myself to be. Where there had been humility there was haughty pride, where there had been gentleness there was anger. I glimpsed resentment and selfishness too. But I refused to avert my eyes, though I felt like I was looking at a portrait of Dorian Gray. Only I knew this image was not who I really was, or at least who I used to be.

Recently I had been thrown into a Bible study group with four other women I met at church. It was, initially, my attempt to be social, and knowing inherently that, whether I thought I was good at them or not, I needed relationships. And these women had become my friends. So I decided to open up and talk to them. I told them what I knew of myself. What I was discovering. I told them my fear of crying, and that I was afraid I was going to cry soon. It was building up inside of me, and I felt as Job did, like I would burst like old wineskin. My friends listened. But they didn't try to make me feel better about my weaknesses. They didn't tell me I was wrong about myself. Rather they were mirroring what I was learning back to me. And I knew where this six-month journey with these women was taking me—or at least a part of the destination.

And one sunny afternoon, I took a walk. I passed a large boulder and sat down on it. It was a chilly day, so no one else was around. It felt like all my life had been hurtling toward this moment. I knew I was going to cry. And I was terrified I'd never stop. But I let myself go. I cried. I cried hard. I went to the depths of my soul and wrenched up everything that was in there. Like going through a dusty old box in the attic labeled "childhood memories" in faded black marker, I was pulling out things I hadn't seen in years. There were even things I'd forgotten. I cried for all the times I hadn't cried before. And more than grieving, I was surrendering too. I released and surrendered to God. And my fear went unrealized; I did stop crying, though I started crying for everything for a while. It seemed that I cried so easily after that first good cry. I guess knowing I could stop made it acceptable, or maybe I was trying to make up for missed opportunity. Whatever the reason, whether it was empathizing with a friend, feelings of sadness, or even gratefulness, my tears were a close companion.

That act of surrender began a year of immeasurable growth for me as a person, as a friend, as a woman who follows God. It was a turning point that was bigger than just giving up my will in the decision I was making with my husband, or even in just being able to cry. That one act of looking clearly at me led to many revelations about myself and about my faith. I began to see God so clearly that I literally couldn't wait to get more of him. I had never before experienced a relationship with God in such a precise, tangible way. I realized the role that my friendships had played. I saw how in my honesty with them about myself and by confessing what I felt and thought to them, I was able to move forward from the place I was in. I saw in triumph how this woman who had been afraid of relationships, even failed at them, now shared life with others in a very authentic way.

I read a story in *People* magazine about a five-year-old girl, Samantha Runnion, who was kidnapped from her front yard. Tragically, Samantha was not found alive, but her kidnapper was captured and convicted. How they found him was quite remarkable. Samantha essentially led the authorities to her killer. When the suspect's car was searched, they swept it for DNA evidence. Samantha's tears were on the door handle of the vehicle, and they held her DNA code. A simple thing like a teardrop holds all the complexities of our DNA. And it holds more; it holds the memories, it holds the pain, it holds the fear. And shedding them can save you. Samantha's tears didn't save her, but they did perhaps save other little girls who might have been her killer's next victims. And my tears saved me in a different way.

As I look back over the last year, I am amazed that the day on the rock was a mere twelve months ago. So much has happened. I know I haven't arrived. I never will until I'm finished with my life on earth. But I hope in the experiences I've had, the things I've learned will provide a little cushion in the next dip. Or perhaps what I now know will make the valleys in my life a little shallower. Maybe rather than life being dips and hills, it will move like a little wave as it ebbs and flows.

Discussion Questions

1. What are your fears? What do you do to avoid facing them?
2. How do you define courage?
3. Do you think you should have less fear if you are a Christian? Why?
4. Do you think you are a courageous person?

10

fairy tales and the real world

S A B R I N A

*Many persons have the wrong idea of what
constitutes true happiness. It is not attained
through self-gratification but through fidelity
to a worthy purpose.*

—Helen Keller

I REMEMBER ONCE WATCHING the movie *Sabrina*. It begins with the words "once upon a time." Sabrina is homely and socially awkward. And she lives in her head. She has great dreams of capturing the resident and rich playboy, who, of course, almost literally doesn't know she exists. But still Sabrina dreams. Then her father decides to send her to Paris for six months, in part because he hopes getting her away will get the obsession of this man out of her heart. He works his connections and sets up a job for her, and away she goes, somewhat unwillingly and still pining after the playboy. But over time she lives, she really lives. And she opens herself up to people, to experiences, to life outside of where she grew up. And Sabrina evolves into a beautiful woman. (I especially love those physical-transformation movies.)

When she returns home, she is gorgeous and glamorous, practically unrecognizable. But one thing has not changed. She is still very much in love with the playboy. She does capture his eye this time, and it seems that all Sabrina's dreams will come true. The man she has always wanted now wants to be with her. But in a plot twist you know is coming but welcome just the same, she falls in love with another man. And you just know they're meant to be together. But of course before they can live happily ever after, he must break her heart. He does. And she leaves. She runs away to Paris, the city where she found herself. But he follows her there and declares his love to her so poetically, so beautifully. They kiss passionately on a bridge overlooking the Seine River in the most romantic city in the world while music plays in the background.

That is the life I dreamt of. Not literally, of course. I wasn't in love with a playboy, and I didn't go to Paris to find myself. But I longed to see the realization of my dreams, to love and be loved, so desperately . . . and being gorgeous and glamorous wouldn't hurt either. As I sat watching that movie I was in a place in my life where anything was possible. I was just entering college, had yet to declare my major, and the world still lay at my feet. Nothing was carved in stone yet. And as the movie ended and I watched the characters kiss, I felt this great sense of hope and expectation for my life. It didn't matter that any story starting off with "once upon a time" should have tipped me off to the fact that it was just a fairy tale.

I was a girl who always played by the rules. From early on I was very obedient. I aimed to please, and somehow I believed that would pay me back in dividends some day. I have been a dutiful daughter, student, friend, employee, wife, and Christian. And I did so because I always wanted to be happy. Ever since I was a little girl I wanted happiness. I had all these ideas of what would make me happy. And they shifted with age. As a child it was being popular, selling the record number of Girl Scout cookies, being pretty, being the teacher's favorite; then it was being popular with the boys, landing a husband, having the right job, having beautiful children and a happy marriage—a hologram of dreams that shifted depending on the angle from which you looked, and ultimately an illusion. In my naiveté I thought happiness was something I could earn. But my life has not turned out the way I expected or wanted. And the happiness that I chased steadfastly has not been captured.

There is a famous French song called "La Vie en Rose." It plays in the movie when Sabrina is in Paris. The song is about looking at the world through rose-colored glasses. And I suppose I have done that too. I know that the rosy hue isn't real, but without the glasses, I'm not too happy with what I see. Sometimes I'm afraid to really look without the rosy hue to make it all go down easier. W. H. Auden said, "We would rather be ruined than changed; we would rather die in our dread than climb the cross of the moment and let our illusions die."[10] I'm afraid that in the face of reality, I'll be looking eye to eye with my unhappiness. But then it is like the film *The Matrix*, I suppose. Once you know another world exists, it's hard to go back to the fantasy, even if the fantasy looks better—or at least easier.

And it makes me consider whether happiness is something we're even supposed to want. Is it something we can hope for or even pursue? I've heard Christians say many times, "God doesn't want us to be happy." And to me that begs the question: does he want us to be unhappy? What *does* he want for us? What are we *supposed* to want for ourselves? Is it joy? I'll be honest, I don't really get the concept of joy. Oh, I know all the right definitions and vocabulary words, and I've read book after book about being joyful. But I don't know how to access it. I don't know how to find that peace when I am in a place I don't want to be, never thought I would be in—or even when I'm merely disappointed. What about contentment? This is also something that escapes my grasp. And often I wonder if there's a fine line between contentment and resignation. Or maybe I'm simply jealous of those who have found contentment when it has eluded me.

And I wonder if other women are unhappy with their lives too. Do others pretend as I do that things are perfect? I think

122

both men and women are unhappy, sometimes for the same reasons, sometimes not, but I think because of the way we're wired as women, unhappiness has the power to permeate our being. Does the fact that it often seems like a favorite Christian pastime to peer into the lives of others and cast judgment represent a pervasive unhappiness that no one wants to talk about? Or is it just me? Were my expectations simply too high? Were my dreams doomed to failure, only I just didn't know it? Let's face it; I set up my dreams against a kissing scene with Harrison Ford and Julia Ormond. There was music playing. French music. French music doesn't play in my world. I'm not even French. Did I take fairy tales like *Sabrina* far too seriously, even when I knew better?

And so maybe my expectations *were* too high. Maybe the way I thought I'd feel was unrealistic. But seriously, why does so much in life seem to disappoint? I was eating lunch at California Pizza Kitchen the other day with a friend, and the waiter was telling us about how he visited a place he'd dreamed his whole life of visiting. Finally, he got to go there, but he found it disappointing. We all ruefully remarked that seems to be the way of lifelong dreams. And I've heard story after story about those without faith looking for meaning in material possessions or success and finding disappointment. The athlete Dion Sanders is one, for example. The story goes that he became a Christian after he won the Super Bowl and ordered a brand-new Lamborghini for himself. He hung up the phone having achieved everything he wanted in life and was hit by a sense of utter meaninglessness.

But what about when you are already a Christian? How do you deal with feelings of meaninglessness? And can't you still dream of things besides heaven? Is the only guarantee you have eternity? What about when you pursue your dreams in good faith, and they still leave you dissatisfied?

And so if that's the truth, then can I accept it? Can I keep unhappiness from saturating my every thought and feeling? How do I not feel that life cheated me? And then what about my expectations of God? Is it true that he doesn't want me to be happy? How much is he willing to save me from my disenchantment? How do I discover joy, how do I capture contentment?

And then I glimpsed contentment. I was in church one Sunday not too long ago and found myself in a place of peace. I was a stranger to that place. I arrived there by a path that I had begun a few days earlier when I'd had a very profound moment. I saw the hand of God in someone else's life. I heard their story of abandonment, poverty, and overcoming the impossible. And while I listened I saw the presence of God in the life of that person, though I had struggled for some time to feel it in my own. The potency of that realization drowned my gloomy cocktail made of cynicism, disappointment, and self-pity that I was swallowing every day. And then in church a few days later I returned to that moment. As the resonance of music enveloped me, the words "You are my desire, no one else will do" settled deep within my heart, where I have tried to hold them since. I am afraid they will vanish again, and I will be left once more with my disappointment.

As the time for communion approached, I began to think about what it would mean for God to be enough. But it involved a death—the dying of my dreams and the breaking down of my altar of happiness. I took the bread and then the cup. I held the tiny cup of grape juice in my hand, and as I lifted it to my lips I drank to death. Tipping my head back, I swallowed the purple juice and felt it slide down my throat and seep into my belly. And then I imagined it trickling down all the way to my toes. I contemplated that death and mourned it.

We don't like death. When my grandfather died I couldn't approach the casket at his viewing. I was afraid I'd remember him dead rather than alive. I want spring, never winter. I hate the barren trees with their spooky, spindly branches. I want beginnings, not endings, Easter, not Good Friday. And yet, someone once told me that she had the privilege of being with someone when they passed away. She said it was a moment equally powerful and profound, similar to being present at the time of life when her children were born. For only through death is life possible. We as Christians should know this truth well, and yet we avoid death. Even the rituals of our culture show that we don't embrace death. We want our loved ones to look alive, and as we once knew them. But in that moment of communion and of death I experienced true life-giving contentment. And I know it was contentment because nothing in my life had changed. When I exited the church my life would look exactly the same as it had when I'd entered. But I was different.

You might think my experience is nothing different than many you have had, but for me it was profound, and for more than one reason. Yes, I've heard many compelling stories before now of how God has worked in someone else's life. But it never really affected me. But to feel contentment in spite of the fact that nothing had changed in my life personally was momentous. The struggles, the disappointment, the stalemates, the silence were still unchanged. And then, to find pleasure in the miracle of another human being while seeing none in my own life was truly unique for me. Instead of feeling sorry for myself and comparing my experiences to theirs, or asking God what I had done wrong, I simply celebrated this obvious presence in someone else. And for that moment that was enough. God was enough. If nothing in my life ever changed, I didn't need or want more. And I wasn't asking for more, probably for the first time in my life.

I don't think that God wants us to be unhappy. And yet, I don't believe happiness is our right either. But I had that experience, that moment of contentment and faith, and I believe that means there can be another and another. They may be far apart. And so maybe I go from moment to moment for now. Maybe it won't always be that way. Maybe it will. But this is real. There's no "La Vie en Rose" playing, and I'm not being kissed on a bridge in Paris. It's me, not pretending or being fake. It's me being honest about my questions and my disappointment and my triumphs, and living that moment as long as it lets me, until I get to the next.

And I still might hang on to a little bit of fairy tale. Though there is death, the death of dreams, out of the ashes the phoenix rises, so the legend goes. For like Sabrina's life, my life hasn't taken me where I wanted to go, but maybe I'll find something special in the places I find myself instead. A girl's gotta dream, right?

Discussion Questions

1. What are your expectations for your life?
2. Have they evolved or changed over time?
3. Where do you think your expectations came from?
4. Do you think God wants us to be happy?
5. Are you willing to admit when life has disappointed you?

11

listening to lies

L EE

*No one can make you feel inferior without
your consent.*

—Eleanor Roosevelt

FEEL LIKE I have a deep, dark secret. That is, I am a fake. Somehow I have succeeded in fooling the entire world, and I've been playing the game since I was a little girl. When I was in elementary school they had this smart kids group. Oh, every elementary school has them. I am convinced they exist to ensure that from a very young age we can feel inadequate or in competition with each other, because I don't think it developed my skills any further than the regular classroom. Somehow I ended up in the smart kids group. This meant that once a week the teacher made an announcement, and we, the smart kids, got to leave our regular classroom and go together to another classroom where we worked on special projects. The thing is, I lived in constant fear that it was a mistake. I didn't know how I had ended up in that classroom, but I was sure it was an accident and eventually the teacher would find out that I was not really that gifted.

When I was in junior high I was asked by my math teacher to compete on behalf of the school in a math competition. Again, I was certain there was some mistake. But I was also too timid to refuse, so I went and I competed, and then I went again and again. And I was terrified, not of the competition but of failing somehow and being revealed as a phony. But I always worked especially hard because I thought I needed to earn the right to stay there and keep everyone from finding out I didn't belong.

I grew up, I went to college, I got married, and I married a man who is very intelligent. I also work in a creative field, and my work is on display for the public. This means that I get feedback from the public on what I present to them. I often receive approval, even applause. And yet I still fear that people will realize that I'm just not that talented. I also still live with the idea that I am not smart. Yes, the third grade still haunts me, and this belief is something I continue to try to hide.

Now as a thirty-eight-year-old adult with four children of my own, I live with the same fears. I still look over my shoulder, convinced someone is going to find me out. But what this also means is that I feel the pressure to keep up the façade. Lest I be exposed, I do things in an effort to play along with the image others have of me.

Growing up, I never developed this confidence, even though as a child I began to experience success. For instance, I loved to paint. Later at the prompting of my mother I started to enter my work in art shows. I remember one day when I spent the morning painting. If the piece turned out as I hoped, I planned to enter it in my first show, so I worked painstakingly. I finished my work and was feeling pretty good about it when my mother called me for lunch. I left the canvas there on the easel. The next day, when I returned to the painting, I recognized brush strokes that were not mine. I knew my own style and technique—and I knew my mother's too. I knew her work and that she had gone back and added to my painting. I'm sure in her mind she thought she'd add a little bit here and there to round out the whole piece and improve it. I'm sure she thought I wouldn't even notice. But I did. Obviously, I felt like my own attempt wasn't good enough. I ended up winning first place in the show. But inside I didn't feel deserving. It wasn't my work. My mother always helped me with every project—writing competitions, science fairs, book reports. I always got first place and received constant praise. Every work I produced was the best. But inside I felt like a fake because it wasn't totally my own work.

131

And my mother was and is a very confident woman. She knew what she liked and disliked, she knew what she wanted, and she knew how to get it. My parents were intelligent, wise, and successful people, and I guess with so much confidence projected at me, how could I develop my own? I just always looked to others for what I thought and for determining the choices I would make.

The truth is, I think some of these things I believe are lies that I tell myself. They are judgment tapes that replay over and over in my mind. It is easier to believe the lies because I lack confidence in who I am and the woman I have grown into. When I look in the mirror I see a grown woman with a beautiful home, a family, a career that enables me to use my talent and even brings me accolades, yet I feel that even my outward persona is part of the charade. When I was a little girl I loved playing dress-up. I had this old trunk that was my grandfather's from when he was in the Navy. It was filled with my mother's old clothes that she didn't wear anymore—dresses, shoes, even hats and handbags. Sometimes my grandmother and my aunts would make contributions to the box too. I'd put on a dress, top it with a hat, slip my little feet into some high heels, and schlep around the house pretending to be a grown-up.

I still feel like I'm playing dress-up, only this time the shoes and dresses actually fit me. Because inside I am still a little girl who wonders what people think of me, and who feels stupid when I trip and people see the misstep. I still want to be popular; I still worry about having "cool" clothes. All the things that I thought wouldn't matter once I was an adult still matter very much, at least to me. But I somehow think that I am the only one who still feels insecure. I know it's probably another lie, but I really believe that other women feel much more self-assured.

I guess I started telling myself these lies, or maybe sometimes I listened to the lies others told me. But the thing with lies is that often there is just a little bit of truth mixed in there. And that's the scary thing about them, and the thing that makes them easy to believe. They wouldn't be effective without that little grain of truth. And when the world confirms the lie, it cuts deep to the core of your soul.

Just ask Janey Karp.[11] Janey is a woman I read about in the paper one morning while sipping my coffee. For years Janey battled depression and anxiety with the help of prescription medications. But Janey was very private about her medication. She was afraid that if people knew she was depressed and needed medication they would think she was crazy or psychotic. One day after filling her prescription for Ambien, a sleeping aid, she read the printout attached to the medication. The printout had a notes page attached that revealed any comments made to her patient file at the pharmacy. There on the printout Janey read the words *crazy* and *psycho*. The notes were typically used internally as a prompting to the pharmacist and were entered into the computer by various staff members. Now Janey was reading them on a computer printout. I imagine her stomach plummeted to her knees and her heart pounded deafeningly in her ears. Her mind probably instantly flashed to all the other people in her life who might think the same thing. Her fears of being stigmatized, being labeled, were realized. The world confirmed her lie.

And I knew the feeling. When my husband and I were getting ready to buy a new car, I did some research. As I told him everything I had discovered, he didn't seem too responsive. Finally he questioned what I said in a way that made me feel stupid. Immediately I felt like I was standing before him as a little girl in pink pajamas with the "footies" in them. *What do I know about this?* I told myself. *He's the man. He knows more about cars and finance, and he's the smart one in this marriage. Who do I think I am?*

When he questioned me I felt almost weak. As if a life force was leaving my body. I knew then that I needed to confront these lies. I knew this because I saw how they hindered me. I saw how they paralyzed me and made me afraid to let people into my life, and afraid to make good decisions with confidence. I knew that without defeating these beliefs I would never be able to be the confident woman that I pretended to be. I knew that I needed to have the courage to look the lies square on and identify what is the truth. I needed to confess them and purge them, perhaps to my husband or to my friends. As I was sitting with my friends one day, I thought about maybe saying some of the things I believed about myself out loud. I thought if I let those thoughts breathe outside of myself they would either die from lack of oxygen or thrive all on their own. And I needed to find out if these lies were parasitic—did they survive only by sucking the life out of me?

But I was afraid I would say, "I think I'm stupid," and they would look at me sympathetically as if to say, "Poor girl, we hoped she'd never realize the truth about herself." Yet I wanted so desperately to fight my way out of the mire of these lies that I was wallowing in. And I knew I couldn't do it alone. So I said the words. I wanted to tell all my lies, but I started with, "I'm stupid." And I did see looks of recognition. But not in the way I thought I would. I saw women whom I thought were so confident and successful look at me with expressions of recognition on their faces because they feared the same about themselves. It was a moment of sheer vulnerability for all of us. There was something about naming those lies—as if doing so held them suspended in the air, waiting to see what I would do next with them.

And it was life changing, because sometimes it seems as if God is where my fear is. And so I often go looking for him there. There's a part of me that wonders if he is trying to show me something that I can see only in the inner recesses of my fears, amid the wrestling, begging, and crying. I find God there in the eye of the storm. It's as if he's waiting for me. But I want that relationship with him, and so it seems that I must go to where I don't want to go—to the center of my fears.

Discussion Questions

1. What are some of the lies you find yourself believing?
2. Where do you think they came from?
3. What needs to happen for you to see these lies for what they are?
4. How do you know when it's a lie and when it's conviction in your own heart?

12

perfectionism

CAROLINE

The thing that is really hard, and really amazing, is giving up on being perfect and beginning the work of becoming yourself.

—Anna Quindlen

WHAT ARE THE images of success? What are the symbols that say "you've made it" or "you're the best"? What makes everyone want to be you? Okay, so maybe as Christians we think of those sorts of questions as worldly. We don't talk about success the same way because we think it's crass, even unchristian. We talk about how the world looks for success, but we know God looks at the heart. And of course it's true that he does. God doesn't have the same expectations for success that we have, and he is unmoved by an award, a promotion, or an expensive car as far as determining value or worth. But though we pay lip service to our worth being in God alone, we do have standards for success. So what are the images of a life well lived? What do you have to do for someone to say at your funeral that God will greet you at the gates of heaven with a big fat "Well done, my faithful servant"? What are the symbols of living a life that is "blameless" or "above reproach" or "honoring to God"? What does it mean to say, "All God wants is your best"?

I'm sure you think I'm misunderstanding something about the Christian life here at best or that I'm terribly cynical at worst. But whether I am correct in what I'm saying or not, it was my perception. And my perception has been slowly and quietly choking me, cutting off my lifeline.

In my first-grade classroom a chart hung on the wall. Every child's name was printed on the orange-colored poster board. In the boxes went stars—green stars for doing what was expected of you, silver stars for going above and beyond, and gold stars for being truly excellent. And then there were those boxes with black marker Xs. Those kids didn't even rate. At the end of every day before dismissal, the teacher would call out our names and give us a star to stick onto the board, or we had to go up to mark an X. And so each day a classroom full of six-year-olds did the walk of fame or shame up to the poster board while the whole world looked on. Because let's face it, in the first grade your classmates are pretty much the whole world.

A gold star was usually beside my name on the chart. Then there were quarterly report cards marked "N" for "Needs Improvement," "S" for "Satisfactory," and "E" for "Excellent." I was always disappointed even with "S." In the fifth grade my Sunday school teacher gave us a statement to tape to our bathroom mirror. It was a self-esteem message that we were supposed to recite every morning. All I remember is the first line, "I am a child of the king." It was supposed to remind us of our self-worth in God regardless of anything else we accomplished. And I did recite it every day—because I always did what I was told. Only I didn't know how to make it feel true. And I continued to add to my cache of external success. There was a blue ribbon in the third-grade science fair, a Girl Scout sash filled with badges, a plaque for the highest grade in biology, and a homecoming crown my senior year of high school . . . those were the childhood symbols of accomplishments, and a quest for perfection.

Before I got to college I stopped eating. I never liked my body, but as I filled out and developed, I began to hate it. I was sixteen when I first started—or stopped, however you want to say it. There were other measures of success besides gold stars and trophies. There was the quest for physical affection and to look like everyone else. No one knew at first, not my family or friends, and that allowed me to continue into college with ease. I got thinner, but I kept a busy schedule so I could avoid eating in front of other people, and no one thought anything of it. Now I was away from home so I didn't even have to be as careful to hide it. And everyone else in college did it too. Or so it seemed. They actually call it the "college girl disease" because so many girls develop it in college dorms and sororities.[12] And at a Christian college it's no different. When I first started, I would occasionally skip a meal because I knew I'd eaten too much the day before. Then it was hardly eating at all and feeling so proud of myself when I resisted my urge to eat, especially when others ate and I was able to resist.

Outside I was the image of perfection. I came from a good family. I was popular, attractive, smart, and had always been the good child and had grown into a young woman with great potential. Yes, I was on track to continue my spree of successes. Let's face it, those were the things that made a family Christmas letter. No one talks about how mediocre their child was that year or what they didn't do.

It wasn't that I was searching only for outward perfection. I had to be successful inside too. Raised to be a devout Christian, I not only had to have all the trappings that would give the outward appearance of accomplishment, I had to examine my heart. I had to "be ye perfect as your heavenly Father is perfect." I was trying to be perfect for my parents, for everyone else, for God, and for myself.

I was brought up in a conservative Christian home in a fairly small town. People in our church were always in everyone else's business. There was certainly a standard for conduct established by "what will people think," and I think it was spiritualized too. Often what was held up as living for God was really about living for others. Or maybe it's just that the judgment of others seems more tangible, loud, and always available. And there were certainly people I knew who messed up. There was the girl in our youth group who got pregnant, there was the high school boy who drank, there was the Sunday night worship leader and the nursery coordinator who had an affair. And they all left the church. Everyone talked about them; they were fodder for family dinner table conversation for months. And even years later if their name would ever come up, it went something like, "Oh, right, yes . . . she's the girl who got pregnant. Oh, she's married, did you say? Well, I'm so glad she found someone who was willing to take her with a past like that."

The movie *Saved* parodied much of the Christian life and met with mixed reviews within the church. Mary is a girl who, in trying to do the right thing, uses some bad judgment and ends up getting pregnant. She doesn't realize that she's pregnant even though she is manifesting symptoms of pregnancy. She is home one night watching a made-for-TV movie with her mother, and the woman in the TV movie thinks she is pregnant and then finds out that she actually has cancer. As she recites her symptoms, it dawns on Mary that she, too, could be pregnant. The next day she hurriedly rides her bike to the drugstore to pick up a pregnancy test. As she peddles furiously home to take the test, she repeats a prayer over and over to herself, pleading with God that it be cancer. The scene is funny. And it's funny because it rings true. Had I gotten pregnant before getting married, I would be pleading for cancer too. Death seemed better than messing up.

And so as a teenager and eventually as an adult I was consumed by what people would think of me. But it wasn't only other people. It was God too. I was terrified at standing at the great white throne and having everyone know my sins. What if my heavenly crown was smaller than everyone else's? Plus, I wanted God to use me to do something for him. I wanted God to bless my life, to give me the desires of my heart as promised, and I thought he would do this only if I was always obedient and always did the right thing. And I guess I loved God because we are supposed to love God. But I was pretty scared of him. I think I saw him like a strict, demanding disciplinarian, and I was always trying not only to meet the mark but exceed it. I always wanted "E," not merely "S." And then there was the worst critic of all. That was me. Sure, I blamed others and the standards set by fear of gossip, failure, and letting others down. But I was the worst taskmaster of all. "We tend to dislike our bodies as we dislike ourselves."[13]

That was certainly true of me. I had waged a full attack on both. Because the truth of the matter is I couldn't love myself if I was imperfect. Oh sure, I knew logically speaking that I had made mistakes before and that I would continue to do so throughout my life, and yet on the other hand I lived as though achieving perfection was possible. I was always doing an internal inventory of my imperfections and would berate myself on how things *should* be. I subjected myself to what Freudian psychologist Karen Horney called in her book *Neurosis and Human Growth* the "tyranny of should."[14] I had a whole laundry list of "shoulds" that needed to purge my reality to make me acceptable. And I thought I was encouraged to do this by my church. We were always reminded to be thinking of ways we had sinned so that we could ask for forgiveness, then look for ways we could improve to be more like Christ. And that is what we are supposed to do. I'm not saying they were wrong, but for a person like me it was a deep burden. I took one truth, obsessed over it, and forgot about other truths—like grace and forgiveness. How can we look at ourselves as people of worth and value and then as wretched sinners too? I'm not asking just to make a point. I'm genuinely asking here. Because I know we are supposed to realize both those things, but I don't know how.

And I did a similar external inventory too. I'd strip down to my bra and underwear, stand in front of my bathroom mirror, and make a mental note of anything I didn't like about my body. I'd pinch an inch here, note a tiny bulge around my back when my bra was fastened on the third hook. I'd take notice of every flaw and determine where I needed improvement. And then I'd hit the treadmill on a mission. There were days when I barely ate and then ran for an hour, pushing myself just a little longer. And I felt so successful as I laid my head on my pillow every night and counted the negative calories. I was destructive to myself from the inside out.

So you see, I was my own worst enemy. And then something happened in my life that I couldn't control. It threatened to out me as not having the perfect life. My failures, my disappointments, and my choices would be out there for everyone to see—and judge. And they were imperfect. And though I tried to control it, to patch the dam break, it was going to leak and everyone would know. And it happened. I was powerless to prevent it, and I was left sitting in my broken attempts to control everything in my life. And it was then that I knew I had a choice. I could pick myself up, brush myself off, chalk it up to someone else's fault, and carry on with trying to be perfect. Or I could embrace my failure as mine, and know that my mistakes didn't define my worth any more than my perfection did.

I had found my worth in my perfection. And I would ask myself, *What thing can I accomplish today to add to my worth?* I see now there is real pride there too. And of course as a perfectionist I find it difficult to admit my faults. To embrace the knowledge that much of my perfectionism is pride and not only insecurity is terrifying. To begin with, it means I have to take responsibility for my pride. I have to admit that I'm not perfect. If my perfectionism were rooted in insecurity, then I could maybe blame others and still feel smug. But pride, pride is an ugly thing within my heart that I must take responsibility for.

And how is my perfectionism pride? I always made the statement that I was a perfectionist, but I didn't expect perfection from other people. I think back to that now and realize that is the most arrogant statement! It was as if I was saying that I was the only one capable of perfection. I don't put that burden on others because I know they could never measure up. Well, how considerate of me! Again Karen Horney confirms this in her book, saying, "For nothing short of godlike perfection can fulfill his idealized image of himself and satisfy his pride in the exalted attributes which (so he feels) he has, could have, or should have."[15]

The ironic thing is that when I first started to discover this about myself I wondered if other people thought I was prideful, and I worried that it was so obvious to others. I was moving toward self-loathing, but then I began to spend time with people, Presbyterians, who talked an awful lot about grace, you know, unmerited favor. Though I had been raised in a Christian home, I wasn't raised Presbyterian, and my denomination didn't focus on grace. We focused more on conduct and holy living. I lost count of how many times I heard "do the right thing" on a given Sunday morning. And I agonized over that mandate.

I never thought that much about grace before. I never thought about it because, truthfully, I didn't really think I needed it. I didn't think I was that bad. Actually, I thought I was pretty great. And I should have been great; I worked hard enough at it. I heard someone talking about how they cried over their sin. That stayed with me for a while. I had never cried over my sin. When I was growing up I had cried to my parents when I was about to be punished, but it had been a very long time since I'd cried over doing something wrong, and I had never cried over my sin before God. I knew I sinned, I just didn't think it was that bad. After all, I wasn't committing any really atrocious sins. I wasn't having premarital or extramarital sex, I didn't smoke, drink, or do drugs, I hadn't had an abortion, or committed any crimes beyond breaking the speed limit. And then I realized that I had committed the worst sin of all. In my quest for perfection and my obsession with how good I was, I had belittled Jesus' sacrifice for me. Though I wouldn't have ever said this, in reality I was living as though I could save myself and that Jesus needn't have died for me. I just didn't think I was that bad. Now, the serial killer or the chronic adulterer, those guys must really appreciate what Jesus did for them. And how thankful they must be. It must be nice to realize how much you've been saved from. Too bad I wouldn't have the opportunity to know. I had made it my chief end to always do the right thing, to live as perfectly as I could.

And then that path of thought has taken me to something else. Why do we live in terror of making mistakes? And moreover, why do we think we can actually avoid making them? As I look over my life I realize the palpable fear that I have lived with over making mistakes. I was sure people wouldn't love me, and far worse, God wouldn't love me, wouldn't bless me, and might even punish me. I was sure that making a mistake could and would ruin my life.

Does that mean sinning should be taken lightly? Absolutely not. But being less than perfect is something that we all are. And if you don't ever make mistakes, how on earth do you learn? I have lived my life in fear of making the wrong choices, scared I was going to have regrets, and often too paralyzed by this fear to make any choice at all. I was so fearful of letting people down, of letting God down.

And perhaps I feared that in part because I looked down on others for their mistakes. I had participated in that dinner table gossip. I allowed the memory of people's past imperfections to come to mind whenever I thought of them. But there is grace available for when that failure inevitably comes, grace for others, and yes, grace for me. Grace exists for all of us whether we live into it or not and whether we show it to others. So since it's there, why don't we grab hold of it?

In the book of Esther, after Esther is chosen to be in King Xerxes's harem, she spends a year preparing to go before the king. That year involved a strict diet and a regimen of oils and perfumes that she immersed herself in for so long eventually the perfume was absorbed into her body and came out of her pores, making her smell pretty amazing, I imagine. We only perfume the surface of our skin, and most of our scents evaporate within hours. Why don't we immerse ourselves in grace so completely that it oozes out of our pores, its essence spreading to everyone around us? What if we emanated the sweetness of grace rather than the bitterness of judgment? It is okay to fail sometimes. It is inevitable. This I know to be true, but to live that is so much harder. Especially when it feels like I'm the only one who thinks that. To find freedom in embracing that I am not and can never be perfect sounds so nice, but it is hard for a person like me who has been a fanatical perfectionist practically since birth. I'm learning that being imperfect doesn't change who I am.

And who am I exactly? I am an imperfect human being like everyone else. I don't always add up to the standard. But it doesn't mean I don't try. I do still try. But I also try not to be afraid of not always succeeding. I failed before, and I survived. I am a daughter, I am a sister, I am a girlfriend, I am a granddaughter, and I am a friend. I have a responsibility to be these things to these people, to be there for them and to show love to them. But I will fail them as surely as I will fail myself. But I will still try. I will ask myself, *Am I a good family member and a good friend? Am I right in my relationship with God? Am I using my mind? Am I using my gifts? Am I being the woman God made me to be?* Because this is my identity, in its triumphs and failures, it is all me. And I cannot be a slave to the opinion of others. My identity is not in my looks, not in the perceptions of others, not in how good I am. But it is a daily battle for me. I still have those perfectionist tendencies; I want to master these tendencies and move on. But something tells me I may never master it, that it is a daily process, and just when I think I'm in the clear, I'll be consumed by someone else's opinion, I'll lose sight of what I know by the warped obstruction of perfection. But then I can go back to what I once learned, what I once knew, and maybe you can remind me too.

Discussion Questions

1. How do you measure whether you are successful?
2. How do you feel about mistakes you have made? Why?
3. Do you think a Christian fears a mistake more than someone who does not profess to be a Christian?
4. Do you think as a Christian you can be aware of your sinfulness and still feel valued as a person made in God's image?

13

control

ANGIE

*A single rose can be my garden, a single
friend, my world.*

—Leo Buscaglia

HAVE YOU EVER noticed that sometimes the exact place
you don't want to go is often where you end up? I know
it sounds pessimistic, but it's true, isn't it? It seems like your
worst fear so often becomes your reality.

I decided I needed a new hobby. It was my New Year's
resolution to find a new activity that I could learn and master.

So I went out and purchased a brand-new mountain bike. Some of my friends had gotten into mountain biking recently, and I thought it would be something we could do together. I researched, and read, and asked people who already owned mountain bikes lots of questions. I did this for a couple of months and finally determined the bike that was right for me. After making the purchase, I needed the accessories too, of course, so I bought a helmet, gloves, and toe clips. (It wasn't until after my first ride that I decided I also needed the bike shorts with the padding on the behind.)

Then we got an unexpectedly warm and sunny day in early March, so I loaded my bike in the back of my SUV and drove out to a trail that ran along the river. After gearing up, I walked the bike over to the entrance of the trail, hoisted one leg over the side of the bike, and slid onto the bony seat. I worked the front part of my foot into my toe clips, and I started to pedal.

Now, I hadn't actually been on a bike for many years. When I first bought this bike I'd ridden it around a parking lot for an hour, but that was the extent of it. I didn't even jump one of those cement parking blocks or anything; the most exciting thing was a speed bump. I'd never in all my life ridden my bike on a trail like this one. The closest I'd ever come to a trail at all was riding across my neighbor's backyard, trying to take a shortcut home from the candy store I'd ridden to after school with my friend. And that was in the seventh grade—a long, long time ago. I wasn't even sure I'd ridden a bike at all since the seventh grade. So I was pretty nervous, but you know the saying, "It's like riding a bike . . ."

152

I pedaled up the trail over tree roots and leaves, sticks, and a few small rocks and pebbles. Then I came to a bridge. It required me to navigate a turn to get onto the bridge, and I had no choice but to do so because that's where the trail went. But I've never been good at turns; they've always scared me, whether I was on a bike, ice skates, roller skates. Now, this bend challenged me to make a pretty sharp turn. And I didn't quite make it. I saw myself going toward the railing on the bridge. I leaned my body to the side and kept trying to execute the turn, all the while looking at the railing in the bridge fearful I was going to ram it. And I did exactly that. I ran into the railing, knocking off the reflector that sat atop my front wheel. And I scratched my bike too. I was not happy at all about this.

I was a little unnerved by my first wreck, and disappointed I had already damaged my brand-new bike, but my friends tried to convince me that it was cooler that way, that no one wanted a shiny, new-looking bike. "It looked too rookie, too amateur," they said. So I shook it off and continued down the path. But after crossing the bridge, the trail narrowed. It was hard to keep the bike on the trail, but the path was deep with high ridges, and off the path it was far too overgrown. I would surely wipe out if I veered off the designated trail. I kept my head down, watching the trail and weaving and wavering, trying to keep on the narrow path. But in the way were steep hills, huge roots jutting from the ground, and large rocks. It was very tricky to navigate without toppling over or being sent splattering to the ground by an obtrusive rock.

The men didn't seem to mind biting the dust occasionally. They even seemed to wear their scrapes and bruises like badges of manhood. But I didn't need to prove I was tough; I needed to not break my neck. But I kept falling anyway. Over and over I spilled every time a large rock got in the way. I couldn't figure out how it was happening. I'd see a large rock or tree root looming up ahead and beside it a narrow strip of trail with which to navigate around the rock or root. I'd direct my bike toward the trail, my eye on the rock to avoid it, but I would hit it every time. Wham! I'd hit it and drop my foot to the ground as fast as I could to avoid falling. I got to where I hated the toe clips and didn't put my feet into them because I couldn't get them out fast enough. The toe clips made me feel trapped, like I would be out of control in a crisis, not able to get my limbs to the ground quickly enough to keep myself, and the bike, from falling. I have to admit, I didn't enjoy the ride—not at all, even though it was a beautiful day. I was so relieved when I saw the end of the trail. The sun was getting a little lower in the sky, causing some of the warmth of the day to steal away. I was tired, sore, and muddy. When I saw my car with its four wheels there in the parking lot a few hundred yards away I wanted to drop my bike and run toward it. It was scary enough to be on the bike because I didn't feel in control. But then add trying to steer the narrow trail and all the obstacles, and mountain biking seemed to be a feat I wouldn't be able to accomplish. I was frustrated by the fact that no matter how hard I tried to avoid those obstructions, I never did. And then the feeling of falling, and not being able to release my feet from the clips to save myself, was really quite terrifying. Overall, I hated the feeling of being out of control . . . so much for adventure.

Later, after returning home, enjoying a hot shower, and taking inventory of my bruises, I thumbed through a book about mountain biking that I'd picked up at the bike shop. I'd spent way too much on that bike to give up after one day. And I read something that surprised me. The book said that when trying to avoid an obstruction on the trail, you should never look directly at the obstacle. The book continued on to say that you will always go in the direction you are looking, not where you think you are pointing the bike. So if you don't want to hit the tree root then don't look at it. In short, keep your eyes only where you want to go, not where you don't. That was exactly what was happening to me out there on the trail. Obviously, bikers have a tendency to focus on where they don't want to go in an effort to avoid it, but according to the book this would ensure going exactly where you didn't want to end up. From my experience, I knew this to be exactly right. And I got to thinking that maybe it was the same with life.

I was a little girl when my parents divorced, and though I remained close to both my parents, the divorce devastated me. I don't know if their divorce had anything to do with it or not, but even as a very young child I feared that people would leave me. I tried to be good at relationships so people would never leave. I have always known myself to be a perfectionist, and I tried to be perfect and make everything around me perfect in an effort to keep relationships from ending, people from leaving me. This even carried over to my job, as I have always tried to be the perfect employee, performing impeccably to avoid getting fired. But I also placed a very high value on other people in my life, my family and friends, and I required the same in return.

Lately I've been in the throes of some soul searching—actually, I've been forced into it by the events in my life of late—and I realize that it's not really perfectionism that is my weakness or what keeps me from being my most effective self. I was okay with being a perfectionist. I mean, I know it's stressful and often neurotic, but at the same time it drove me to be a good employee and a good friend. You get measurable results from being a perfectionist. But I am starting to realize that it's not perfectionism that is my problem, rather it is control. And that doesn't sound nearly so good. Nobody likes a control freak. It's like in a job interview when they ask you what your weakness is, you're supposed to say something like "I'm a perfectionist" or "I work too hard." If you said, "I'm overly demanding and very difficult to work with," you probably wouldn't get the job. Well, I realize I am about control, and it is not a label I like.

To begin with, I am afraid of not having control of my own happiness and the things that will bring me this happiness. I mean, who doesn't want to be happy, right? But I realize that I always put my happiness in other people's hands. Which is ironic because then it seems that I have less control. And actually that is what has happened, only I didn't realize it until recently. I thought that by being the perfect friend I could guarantee that I would never be left, that all my needs would be met, and that I could look to my relationships to give me my sense of self-worth. I thought I could depend on the people in my life to pick me up when I was down and generally bring me happiness, but I put all my eggs in one basket, so to speak.

The truth is I didn't want to let God control my life. I know that as Christians we are supposed to want that, but I was afraid if I did that I wouldn't get what I really wanted out of life. I was sure if I relinquished control I would end up a missionary, single and alone in Africa. So I set out to control my own happiness, and I tried to win this through the people in my life.

I wanted the whole dream, to have the husband, the house, the kids. I thought that would bring me happiness. Most people want those things, don't they? And most people get them too. But in my quest for happiness I married a man I should not have married. And even though a voice inside me told me I was wrong, I pushed the voice away, determined I could make it work, that I could make him love me enough. And from the beginning the marriage was wrong. It didn't bring me happiness, it didn't bring me fulfillment, and it didn't solve my problems. It actually created more. I saw my dreams slipping out of my hands, but I didn't want this relationship to end. This was the very thing I didn't want. I desperately didn't want to get divorced like my parents, and so I was determined to make it work. But it didn't. Maybe because it was wrong all along or maybe I focused too much on where I didn't want to go. Divorce loomed like a dark and violent storm coming, and I began to realize I could not control my marriage or my husband.

And so my marriage ended, and I was devastated. But it wasn't only my failed marriage that broke my heart, it was the fear that I might never have the things in life that I so desperately wanted—people to take care of me, to make me feel valued and special, and yes, happy. I began to look for love and significance in other people and began a lifestyle that was harmful to me. Then to add to the woes of my personal life, I was in a dead-end job that I hated. I had just gotten divorced, I was falling into and out of more hurtful relationships, and I was struggling to make it financially on my own. My life was spinning out of control, and I felt powerless to get a foot down to stop myself.

I know it's a cliché, but so often you hear Christians talk about how they were always trying to control their lives until something happened that was out of their control and they had no choice but to turn to God. And that is what happened to me. Finally I threw up my hands and said, "Okay, God, you just tell me, because I don't have a clue." And I began voraciously trying to discover God's purpose for me so that I could do his will. I studied the Bible, read book after book about knowing the will of God, finding your purpose, and living the life you were created to live, and I asked questions of everyone I thought could help me—and even some who couldn't.

And God did meet me in my need. When I released that control, things systematically began to change. One event happened that changed my entire life. I got a new job, which turned my finances around, and I made new friends who were supportive and empowered me to step away from the self-destructive way I had been living my life. Even now it still amazes me to look back and see how God worked in my life. I could have never brought that about on my own, of that I am certain.

But regaining my life also helped me regain control of it. It put me back on my feet and gave me the freedom to live life on my terms again. And again I chose to put how I felt about myself, the measure of my success, and all my needs heaped high on the people in my life. And I know, of course, my expectations are impossible to meet. Again I seemed to set myself up for failure, and so now I am once again in a place of no control.

Circumstances have come together in such a way that now I feel completely alone. Relationships have broken, friends have let me down, I have let them down, people are busy, and inevitably the mess of their own lives is all they can tackle. But I do not want to be alone. I'll say it again for emphasis: *I do not want to be alone.* That is the last thing I ever wanted—again! And now here I am.

Okay, so here's where I am supposed to throw my hands up and ask God to be in control. Now is the time when I am supposed to lean on God. Only this time it seems harder to relinquish control. People say that when you let God be in control, great things start happening. But if I give up control just so God will do these supposed great things in my life, then how am I not still trying to control? I am still trying to control the outcome, thinking I can fool God by pretending to remove my death grip around my life and my future just to get him to step in and take control. And then I'll just wrestle it back from him again anyway after he sets everything right. I know myself. I have spent so much of my life trying to discover God's purpose for me. But I think I was doing all of that just so I could gather a little more information with which to continue to control my life. It was as if I was pumping God for information I could use. It was like insider trading or something (and we know what happens to those people!). It was no different than refusing to keep my feet in the clips and just ride.

And this time I'm angry too. That's the other thing that makes turning over control difficult. I'm pretty ticked. If God created us for relationships, why do they continue to hurt us? We know that we are only human, and that we will fail. So what are we supposed to depend on people for anyway? Are we just supposed to be content with God? It's just not the same; I'm sorry, but it's not. God doesn't audibly speak to me. I can't physically feel God, I can't touch him, I can't see him light up into a smile when I walk into a room. If I were to physically lean on God I would fall over, but I can lean my head on someone's shoulder and feel their arm around me, and that just feels so good. How do I get out of my relationship with God what I can get out of earthly relationships? Am I even supposed to try?

Sometimes we may view God like a mean older brother. We say that God won't give us what we desire until we don't want it anymore. This reminds me of my own older brother when I was little. He would take away one of my favorite toys and hold it high over his head where I couldn't reach it. I'd try everything to get it from him, jumping onto the furniture to try to gain some height, even resorting to kicking him, and then finally crying. But no matter what I did, he wouldn't budge. I'd finally get my toy back when I'd give up and the game became boring to him. I learned eventually to act like I didn't care, and he'd quickly tire of torturing me. Is that how it is with God?

Someone told me about a girl they knew who wanted so desperately to get married. The only thing she wanted from life was to be a wife and mother, and she was a good person, a strong and committed Christian. She talked all the time about wanting a husband, and she was earnestly praying. She decided to enroll in seminary, hoping to gain some further education and land a husband. Everyone knows that seminaries are teeming with men looking for a wife who will assist them in their ministry, and this girl actually wanted to be in the ministry. Someone once asked her why she was going back to school. She quipped, "To find a husband." The person who asked the question told her that God would never give her a husband until she released that desire to him. The girl was undeterred. And off she went to seminary, and wouldn't you know it, in a matter of weeks she met a man and fell in love.

They were married quickly, and within months he was diagnosed with cancer and died shortly afterward. I don't know how this girl handled it. I don't know if it tested her faith, if it made it paper thin or strong like steel. I know positively that

God has a plan for this woman, and that he loves her more than we can imagine. Not ever having been in her situation, I don't know how I would react, but I can guess that I would be asking God why. And I probably wouldn't be too polite about it. I also wonder if I'd feel scammed, like finally my dreams were coming true and then, poof, they vanished. If I gave up control, I would be afraid to really enjoy something, to really love and trust, because if I didn't live the way God wanted, he'd take it away from me. Every good thing that happens I expect the bottom to drop out.

I think I know why circumstances have come together this way. I know what I need to do. I know in my heart what is right for me. I need to trust and to have faith—in God. And I think I can; I think I can get to that place, but I also want to yell at him and say, "Okay, I give in. I'll trust you to meet my needs, but you've got to step up to the plate. Don't leave me hanging out here alone." I have to let my faith overtake my fear. This I know. But that's the hard part, that's the struggle. I'm not all the way there yet.

When I read in the mountain biking book about not looking in the direction you don't want to go, it made me think of another story. The disciples were in a boat on the lake. Jesus had sent them on ahead of him because he needed some time to rest and to pray. When he went to join them again, it was a windy night, and he found them far from shore, struggling in the boat being battered by the waves. And so he walked out to them—on the water. When they saw him, understandably they were terrified and thought they were seeing a ghost.

But when Jesus saw the disciples were afraid, he immediately called out to them and reassured them it was he, in the flesh. He told them not to be afraid. Then Peter asked for reassurance, saying to Jesus, "Lord, if it's you, tell me to come to you on the water."

Now, what was Peter thinking at that moment? What if it wasn't Jesus? As soon as he stepped into the water he would sink. Was he calling Jesus' bluff? I think it's doubtful. I think he just had faith, and maybe he felt a little invincible in that moment, still basking in Jesus' miraculous power. After all, right before they climbed in the boat, Peter had witnessed the feeding of five thousand people with only five loaves of bread and two fish. Why else would you step out of a boat that was being tossed by large waves? They could barely row the craft; he wasn't going to be able to swim in those waves and wind. But Jesus said simply, "Come." There were no further instructions, no "Put this leg in the water first," no "Walk like this." So Peter just got out of the boat. I wonder what it felt like. Did he stretch his arms out to either side? Did he sink down even a little so that just his toes were immersed in the water? Did the water feel firm? Was it easy to walk on, or did it feel like one of those dreams when you're trying to run but your feet feel so encumbered you can hardly move?

So Peter began to walk on the water toward Jesus. He was actually doing it! And he was gaining; he was closing the distance between himself and Jesus. And then he had a moment of fear. I guess Peter was like all of us—just when you get your heart and your head right, you lose a little ground, like the saying "three steps forward, two steps back." And Peter began to worry about the water. And in that moment of trepidation, the very thing he feared began to happen. He started to sink. He cried out in desperation to be rescued, and Jesus reached out his hand and pulled him up. After he caught Peter, Jesus asked him, "Why did you doubt?" And then together they climbed into the boat.

Discussion Questions

1. Do you think it's possible to never feel loneliness?
2. What expectations do you put on the people in your life to meet your needs?
3. How do you determine when you have let someone down? How do you determine when they have let you down?
4. What do you try to control? What would happen if you stopped trying?

14

knowing my personal truth

TRI CIA

If you have knowledge, let others light their candles in it.

—Margaret Fuller

OW DO YOU know when you know? How do you have the confidence to know you are capable of making a decision?

Many of the women with whom I am friends take a bystander approach to their lives. Their husbands make all the major decisions. In buying a home, purchasing a car, investing in retirement, his job change, and budget matters they feel completely comfortable sitting out the game and merely rooting from the sidelines. But I'm wondering is this because they really don't care and so they are comfortable leaning on their husbands, leaving those decisions up to him, or do they just think they can't make those kinds of decisions—either because they don't feel it is their biblical role or because they don't feel confident in their ability to make big decisions? Is it about confidence in someone else or lack of confidence in themselves?

I'm certainly not being critical of them. They are my friends. And there was a time when my life looked an awful lot like theirs. I didn't trust my ability to think critically, to draw from my experience, to learn something that intimidated me, and to know what my gut was telling me. And I am not leaving God out of the picture. I very much wanted to do what God wanted me to, but instead of thinking he would and could speak directly to me, even through me, I always looked to know his will by how others advised me.

I am very close to my family and always have been. My brother, my only sibling, is barely a year older than me. I began to notice from the time we were young the way we were raised differently because of our gender. I think the fact that we were so close in age created a discrepancy that was more obvious. To begin with, I always had to help Mother with dinner. I ripped lettuce and washed tomatoes for salad, filled the bread basket, set the table, poured drinks, and called my father and brother to the table. My brother was usually out playing basketball with his friends or watching TV. After dinner I helped my mother clear the table and clean up. When we were older, my brother had a later curfew than I did. He was also permitted to date before I was and to learn to drive at the legal age, while I had to wait a year beyond that. Sure, I got frustrated at times. I whined that things weren't fair, but I didn't resent my brother. My parents explained many of the differing standards by saying that as a girl my physical safety was at risk. And it's certainly true—later curfews, dates, even driving alone late at night were and are riskier for women. I accepted this, but I didn't like it.

I always obeyed my parents; I was a very obedient child, and that continued into my teenage years. I was raised not to smoke, drink, have premarital sex, or talk back, and I complied with all the rules. Though, admittedly, the sexual abstinence was more out of fear than moral conviction. I'd heard all the talks, warnings, and threats. And I was duly convinced that I would get pregnant the very first time I had sex. And I could never disappoint my parents that way, so I would need to have an abortion. But I knew I could never handle the emotional toll of having an abortion. For that reason I never had sex before I was married.

And I fully trusted my parents. I knew they were good people and devout Christians, and I knew they loved me. I trusted that God spoke through them, and I trusted their decisions completely. In high school I broke up with my boyfriend at their recommendation—and they were right. But as my brother and I got older, I saw even more differences in the way we were guided and advised. While my father was loving and supportive

167

of me, he gave my brother career guidance that he never gave me, he pushed him to achieve more than I was ever encouraged to do. It wasn't that my parents didn't encourage me; they were very emotionally supportive. I just think they didn't consider drive and success, even responsibility, as important because I was probably going to get married and have children, whereas my brother would support a family. I went to college where they wanted me to go and took their advice in choosing my major. And even in college I never dated men they wouldn't approve of. If I couldn't bring him home to Mother and Daddy, I never even went out on a first date. I would have never dreamed of marrying a man they didn't approve of.

Eventually, I married a wonderful man whom my parents thought very highly of. Even so, I sought my parents' wisdom in every major decision. And everything always turned out okay. I wasn't strong-armed or pressured or even controlled by them. I genuinely wanted to do what they thought was best. It was through them that I heard the voice of God, after all. And I wanted to do and be what I thought God wanted.

My inability to have confidence in my decisions became markedly obvious several years after I was married and my husband and I were looking to buy our first house. We settled on a house we liked and began the offer and negotiation process. With every decision we considered, I snuck off and called my parents. They would ask questions and tell me what to look for and what questions I should be asking. I would go back to my husband and ask the questions as if they were mine, not ever telling him I was getting coaching from my parents. Then after I got satisfactory answers, I would take those back to my parents and get more information from them. This went back and forth, and my husband never knew.

Not only did I feel the need to get advice and approval from them on the decisions we were making, but I didn't even stop to think for myself. I never gave consideration to what *I* thought. It's not as if my husband wouldn't have listened to my opinions; he would have. I just didn't trust what I knew. I'd never bought a house before, I reasoned, and besides, my parents had a direct line to God. At least that's what I believed. But my behavior was ridiculous—I see that now. My parents hadn't seen the house, they didn't know what we were looking for, they didn't know the area. They had never even been to that city! I knew enough, but I didn't give myself credit. And more importantly I didn't trust that God could speak directly to me. Rather than seek the answers for myself, I just depended on someone else to tell me, riding the coattails of their spirituality.

Over the next six years I had three children. Then I got pregnant again. In the first trimester my doctor told me that the baby had a severe genetic disorder. They recommended a termination. It was an abortion, but they didn't call it that. I was devastated and afraid. I knew it was an abortion, I knew that inherently, and though it made practical sense, it felt wrong to me. But I was unsure of my judgment and was swayed by what the doctor said. He had made a compelling case, my husband was convinced, but still there was something holding me back. I went to my parents for advice and counsel, and they told me I had no choice but to go ahead with the procedure. I went to my husband's parents, and they supported the doctor as well.

As though searching for someone I trusted to back my feelings and let me off the hook, I went to my pastor. He told me that God had already made the decision when he allowed the baby to develop such a severe disorder. He told me there was really no decision to be made; I simply had to do what was already determined. But locked away inside my soul I felt that it was the wrong choice for me. I had always feared an abortion, knowing the destruction it would wage on my heart. And yet everyone I trusted, my parents, my husband, my pastor, my doctor, was telling me to go ahead. Once again I was afraid to trust what I knew to be true for me because I felt like I was standing alone. And principles can be lonely and unnerving places on which to stand all on one's own. I felt like I was in one of those focus groups you hear about where they test the progression of peer pressure. You know, they hold up a square, for example, and everyone else but the test subject agrees that it's a circle. More often than not, the one on the outside of the scheme folds because he or she begins to question themselves. Only the stakes in my situation were much higher.

I didn't look to myself and to what God was telling me. I looked outside to others. And I put confidence in their titles and degrees, in their godliness, even in their age, banking on the adage "older and wiser." So I terminated my pregnancy. I did what everyone else told me to do. And I was sorry. I am so truly sorry even to this day. The pain of that experience has perhaps diminished some. But it has not disappeared. It never will. To this day my parents refer to the abortion as a miscarriage; to my in-laws it was a D & C, a medical procedure. But to me, I aborted my child—my baby—because something was wrong with her. I know I would have loved her anyway for as long as she lived and beyond. I love her today even though I never met her.

My parents and even my friends tell me I had no choice; they tell me it was indeed a miscarriage. But I get angry when they tell me that. I know I have committed a sin, and I'm not afraid to admit it. I know I stand before God alone and account for my sin. I don't need someone to lie to make me feel better. I think perhaps I leaned so heavily on others to make decisions for me because I thought then there would be someone else to blame if things went wrong. Or at least that I wouldn't have to take responsibility for myself. But when faced with the truth of what I'd done, I didn't lay blame on anyone else. I didn't want to. I had only myself to blame.

But I learned something vitally important too. Something that forever changed me. And that is this: no one knows your personal truth. That is between you and God. No one can tell you. Of course, they can tell you what's in the Bible, they can tell you their opinion, they can give wise counsel. But no one knows your personal truth like you do. And much of the counsel people give is based on their own experience and what God has shown them. Am I saying you shouldn't ask for advice? Not at all. I still ask, and at times I still follow. But there are things that I know that maybe others in my life, whom I respect and trust enormously, don't know. And I know only because of my own personal experiences. I would not judge another who made the same choice I did, but for me it was not the right choice. Many times our experiences are different from one another. Not only in circumstance and detail, but in the way God speaks and even in the way he is present. I think it speaks of his very individual relationship with each of us.

Now, I know my sin, I know my experience, and I know I have a personal relationship with God. I think you have to trust yourself. But of course, trust in self gets you only so far. And so God sends his Holy Spirit to you. And then you know. And you trust. You can trust without knowing the ending. You can trust when things don't turn out the way you thought they would or when the results aren't what you wanted. And for me there is pain in that truth. But pain has made me stronger. And that strength has given me the confidence to know that I know.

Discussion Questions

1. Do you still believe you're right when others disagree with you?
2. Is there anyone in your life whose knowledge you always depend on? Why?
3. Do you think knowledge or experience is more important?

15

living from my soul

SHERRY

I know with certainty that a man's work is nothing but the slow trek to rediscover, through the detours of art those two or three great and simple images in whose presence his heart first opened.

—Albert Camus

THINK MUCH OF a woman's power lies in the fact that she is relational. Talk to any average woman. She probably has a number of close friends, and if she doesn't, then she at the very least still desires those relationships. And there is real emotional intimacy there. That is what we all want—to know and be known.

Our ability to relate to others and the importance we give to relationships gives us our power as women, or more importantly it gives us much of our significance. Whether that is right or wrong, I don't know, but at least that is the case for me. I'm sixty-one years old and have lived many places in my lifetime. And I have friends from all of those locations. People whom I have known for many years that I still keep in touch with and still visit when I have the opportunity.

People and relationships are so important to me. I ask many questions and am genuinely interested in why people do what they do and how they think. I am interested in each person's own story—because everyone has one. Recently at a party I met a gentleman who had made a job change. I engaged in conversation with him wondering why he made the change, why he's happy in the change, why he chose what he did. I'll most likely never see that man again, but I wanted to know more about his story.

And yet often I find myself in conflict with the very thing that gives me this strength. My desire to make people happy drives so much of what I do. But many times the person I am inside is incompatible with the responsibility I feel to those I'm in relationship with—my parents, my brothers and sisters, my husband, my children, even my friends. And I find myself having to choose.

I guess it's because I'm a people pleaser. I have been my whole life, and I have been raised to be that way. I was taught at a very young age that keeping those around me happy and satisfied was supreme. And keeping people happy has meant different things along the way. First, when I was a small child, it required being well behaved and obedient; then it was toeing the line, obeying the rules, and making good life choices; later it meant meeting physical needs, cooking healthy and delectable meals, picking up the dry cleaning, helping with homework; and at every stage it required being flexible and giving up my own will. I felt the pressure to please so intensely that I nearly panicked if I anticipated that I would upset someone by something I chose to do or not to do. I thought like most women my age do, that we come last, whether that is detrimental to us or not.

But as I've gotten older, I have gotten a little braver too. With each passing decade I take a few more chances, I speak my mind a little more frequently, and I do slightly more of what I want to do. But the reality is that I still aim to please. I still struggle with maintaining the traditional role of a wife, daughter, mother, housekeeper, and hostess, though I am a very untraditional person and I hate conformity. And yet, I still feel strongly compelled to do all that those roles require, or at least used to require in the generation I was raised in—cooking, keeping a spotless house, doing laundry, ironing, being available at any time to meet the needs of my husband and children. The thing is, I'm not good at many of those things. I never have been, and with the exception of being available and present, I don't think most of those things are really all that important. Oh, sure, they have to be done, but having kitchen floors one could eat off of has never been something I felt the aspiration to achieve. Nevertheless, I have a large house and many out-of-town friends and family, so this provides a steady stream of overnight visitors. I pour myself into those visits, making nice meals, guiding interesting conversations, planning an assortment of entertaining activities. Before they arrive at my home I pore over recipe books, go to the grocery store, and buy everything I think they would enjoy. I research activities that we can do while they are in town, and I clean my house from top to bottom to ensure that my guest has a wonderfully pleasing visit. And I guess that's called being a good hostess.

But the things that are important to me often come into conflict with my need to make people happy. I would rather have conversation and spend time with people than clean my house. Once when my mother was visiting, we spent the morning looking through old recipes and decided we would make a few of our selections that we resurrected from the "good old days." It was late morning, and I was in my sweats and hadn't showered yet. We were going to run to the grocery store to pick up the ingredients we needed, and as I went to get my coat and shoes my mother looked me up and down and asked, "Are you going to go out looking like that?"

Now anyone with a mother knows that wasn't a question that she expected an answer to. That was her way of telling me she thought I wasn't fit to be seen in public—with her. I didn't want to change. I didn't care, I just wanted to go out and get our groceries. But I knew that if I insisted on doing things how I wanted to, she would be upset. And true, it is a small concession and one that I chose to make for her. But the truth is that over time I have sold myself out to keep peace. And sometimes I feel that I am being so flexible, I am stretched so far that I feel like that little green Gumby figure my son used to play with. I guess because often I'm doing all these things for others, but for the wrong reasons—out of fear and obligation.

I was raised in a large family with four brothers and sisters. My family was very devout, very conventional, and very Southern. We didn't drink, didn't play cards, and didn't listen to rock music. And I was practically raised on clichés, from "children should be seen and not heard" to "don't upset the apple cart" to the "Golden Rule." We ate dinner together as a family every night, and if the preacher came to dinner, I wore my best dress and was on my very best behavior. And for the most part I truly was the good girl; I was an absolute Goody Two-Shoes. I hated conflict and avoided it at all costs. I learned not to ask questions, as it was seen as questioning authority. And since I had such a large family, there were many people to please. But deep down inside, even then, I knew I was different from the rest of my family. I knew I wanted more out of life and relationships than mere conventionality. I didn't just want to toe the line and do what everyone expected. And I had ideas that were different from those of most of my family. They weren't wrong, only different. Hidden away within myself, and though steeped in orthodoxy and generations of conformity, I was a free spirit.

Letting my free spirit out made other people unhappy, and so I had to choose. And I was too afraid to choose myself. As a child we took family vacations every summer. My father always organized them and ran us on a very tight schedule. You can imagine the authority he must have wielded to keep five children on a schedule. I remember when I saw the Grand Canyon for the first time. Even as a child I was in awe. I felt as though I wanted to stand there all day and take it in. But my father wanted to spend five minutes at one overlook then move on to the next destination. Do you know how many overlooks there are at the Grand Canyon? But we could see only one and for minutes. I was crushed. If we stopped to look at a stream or waterfall, I wanted to stick my toes in until they were so numb and red they hurt, but we had to go. We always had to move on and stick to the schedule.

I, on the other hand, have always struggled to keep a schedule. I just don't think it's that important. Often other things get in the way of meeting a deadline or getting to a destination, and if you don't stop to appreciate those "nuisances" I think you miss out. I don't think you're living life to the fullest. Even as a child I felt this sense of desperation, like I wasn't living life completely, like I wasn't going to get to do everything I wanted with my life. I wanted to experience everything. Like a child who won't go to sleep when her parents are throwing a party, I was sure I was going to miss out on something.

And I think that is the larger point for me. It isn't just about the fact that I don't want to clean my house, that I have other ways I want to spend my time. It is figuring out how to be a person yearning to live a certain way but not doing so. How do you know when to live for yourself? Is there ever a time? My kids are grown and have moved out. Is now my time? On the other hand, I still have my husband to make happy. And what about my friends? What does it mean to live life to the fullest? And how do you do that when the life you actually live doesn't support the life you want to live? The life you feel compelled to live? I just don't know. As I have gotten older I have gotten more and more comfortable speaking my mind, and I can be honest about this now—I just don't know. I don't know a whole lot of things!

Last Christmas, or I guess it was advent really, I was at church on Sunday morning. The pastor read from the passage in Luke 1:46.

> And Mary said,
> "My soul glorifies the Lord,
>   and my spirit rejoices in God my Savior,
> for he has been mindful
>   of the humble state of his servant.
> From now on all generations will call me blessed,
>   for the Mighty One has done great things for me—
>   holy is his name.
> His mercy extends to those who fear him,
>   from generation to generation.
> He has performed mighty deeds with his arm;
>   he has scattered those who are proud in their in-
>   most thoughts.
> He has brought down rulers from their thrones
>   but has lifted up the humble.

He has filled the hungry with good things
    but has sent the rich away empty.
He has helped his servant Israel,
    remembering the merciful
to Abraham and his descendants forever,
    even as he said to our fathers."

This passage is called "the Magnificat," or if you prefer the dumbed-down and far less aesthetic title we sometimes use in certain translations, "Mary's Song." Well, how many times had I heard that passage? I told you my age, Christmas comes once a year, you can do the math and get the idea. But something about it held my thoughts in a different way that day, and I let my mind linger there for a while. It never ceases to amaze me how I can read a verse in the Bible so many times that it is almost banal to me, and then it surprises me one day when it finds its way to a different chamber of my heart, bringing it to life. Or maybe *it* actually brings *me* to life.

I contemplated the passage, but mostly I dwelled on the first line, "My soul glorifies the Lord." And then I narrowed it even more until it was just "My soul." Did my soul magnify or glorify the Lord? Did my soul do much of anything? There was something about Mary that I couldn't relate to (well, okay, there were a lot of things). But I wanted to magnify from my soul. I wanted to live from my soul. But why didn't I? Why couldn't I?

And so I thought about that for a long time, and there were many truths I came to realize. There were questions that remained too. I realized that I am too caught up in things that don't matter. Like the average American Christian I am so easily distracted. I think about what I am going to wear—I think about this every day. I think about my happiness or my unhappiness. I think about how I want to be entertained because I am easily bored; I need to watch movies, go out to eat in restaurants, spend time with my friends, work on my hobbies, and spend time with my family. I think about what I need to do for others to make them happy, which will make me feel good—or if not actually good, then at least not guilty. And let's face it: people like to have people pleasers around. I get caught up in being busy and running on the proverbial treadmill, and that creates more frustration. I don't read the Bible with any sense of reality. I don't read it like it counts for eternity. I am more discouraged by the fact that I don't get it. I try to make myself read through the Old Testament, and I stall out, and early on too. I never even make it to Deuteronomy. I read Revelation, and I'm both terrified and confused.

That brings me to another reason I haven't been able to live from my soul. I am not comfortable with mystery. I want to know. I've admitted that I don't know a lot, but I'm not at peace about that. I so desperately want to know much more about so many things. But God is mysterious; often his Word, his actions, even his promises are mysterious. Take something like Proverbs 3:33: "The LORD's curse is on the house of the wicked, but he blesses the home of the righteous." It seems that verse means that good things happen to good people and bad things happen to bad people. I think we can all think of seeming exceptions to both of those. What about the very committed couple at my church who lost their daughter in a car accident? Or how about the woman in my neighborhood who gave so much to others, volunteering in the community, donating her time and money? Then she got cancer. Or look at Proverbs 11:8: "The righteous man is rescued from trouble, and it comes on the wicked instead." Again, it seems that things don't work out quite that way. What about the Christian servicemen who are killed in war, or the good people who were killed on September 11 or in Hurricane Katrina?

Yet I believe God's promises are true, and there are probably a great many times when I am rescued from events and circumstances that I don't even know about. And so hence the mystery. There is the mystery of relationship, intimacy, and even circumstances. But I'm not content in the haze of mystery. I always try to crack the code. And I think that if I am to live from my soul, I must dwell in a little mystery, even embrace it. Or at least accept it. I don't always have to know the answer.

There are three Gospels, Matthew, Mark, and John, that tell the story of the woman who broke the alabaster jar of perfume over Jesus' feet. The perfume she used was extremely expensive. It was so valuable that people often used it as an investment, buying it then reselling for a greater profit. And not only did this woman use the perfume for Jesus' feet, she actually broke the jar and used all of the perfume. She couldn't hold any of it back to keep for herself, or to keep for later. She didn't hold anything back in her expression of love for Jesus. But I hold back all the time. I hold back with others, and I certainly hold back in my love for God. I can't live from my soul when I am keeping part of myself back.

I don't glorify the Lord from my soul, because I often miss seeing his hand in my life. Oh, I think it's there, but I am too caught up with looking at other things that I am doing or that I think God should be doing. Or I worry too much, comparing his hand in the lives of others to what he does or doesn't do in my own life. I feel sorry for myself when I see good things happening to others. If I'm truthful I have to admit I even begrudge them those things when I don't have the same good things in my life. And these are people I care about, yet I struggle to be happy for them.

I think I have missed seeing his hand because my own hands are too full with my burdens and disappointments. Over the years I have stacked the rubble from brokenheartedness or disillusionment, hurt, and regret, and now my pile is stacked so high I can't see over the top of it anymore. It obstructs my view, and I can't see what God is doing and so I can't be driven to live from my soul, worship from my soul, love from my soul.

So what does living from my soul look like? I don't have all the answers to that, but I think that I have to be open to the mystery or else I will miss something. It's like what I said about schedules. If I'm not open to the interruptions in my plan, I might miss out on an experience that could forever stay with me. But to start, at least, there are a few things that I think describe what it means to live from your soul. I think it means embracing what God has given us in the world he has created. I mean really embracing. I want to know every bird call and how they are different and why they are different. I want to feel the wind tickle my skin, or the sun warm my face. I want to stand so close to a waterfall that it is so loud I can't hear anything else. I want to see the sun set over the ocean, dancing on the darkening water; I want to see it from the top of a skyscraper and watch its reflection in the windows of the other buildings. Appreciating the world around us is a part of understanding God's awesomeness, and without glimpsing his creation and taking it in, how can I magnify from my soul?

I also don't live with a sense of urgency. I don't live like each day counts, like it matters. I don't live like life is short. My parents used to have a plaque in their home that said "There is only one life, twill soon be passed." It's not exactly a happy thought, but it's true nonetheless. And I don't live like my life affects my future, that is, my future meaning my afterlife. I busy myself with trying to make my life better here on earth. It's a never-ending quest. And for what? Do I feel God's pleasure in this? Do I delight in him; do I really delight that much at all? Living without that sense of urgency makes everything I do less effective, and yet I still keep doing the same things.

I go back to the Bible, I read of Daniel, of David, of Joseph, and I look at their deep and soulful relationships with God. And they were men! This is what I'm good at doing; I'm good at relationships. So why don't I have the one I want to have with God? Does God cherish me the way he cherished David? Probably not. But David lived from his soul. And God called him a man after his own heart. I am a woman; we want to be cherished. And I want to be cherished like David was.

I really need to be free to be myself. If not with everyone, then I need to spend more time with the people in my life who I can be real with and not be afraid. I have a few people in my life like that, and though it's a short list, I know I'm lucky because some people never find anyone. So why don't I do that more?

How do I live from my soul when the floors need mopping, or I'm doing the "white glove" test to get ready for my mother's visit, or when my husband gets frustrated with me because I forgot to pick up his shirt from the dry cleaner? Are those the priorities, and then I'll live from my soul later? I don't think so. Because you can't live your life thinking, *If I just do this, then I'll live my life*. I'm old enough to know life will pass you by. Is it a balancing act? I guess it is.

But back to my earlier question of how to live what you know is true, when often the container of your life doesn't fit with what you have discovered. The truth is I don't know the answers exactly, but I'm on a journey to discover, or at least try to discover.

But there is this: I have a longing to know God, to magnify him in my own capacity, a longing for him to meet me in a way that fits with me and is true to my natural rhythm and essence—what he has created in me. So I do only what I can. I lay that longing open, I fall into it, and I hope that God shows up to catch me. And if he doesn't in the way that I expect, do I disbelieve? No. I can't. I can't disbelieve, because I do know

God to be true. And I am determined to love wholly from my soul with the purpose of living for God, for that is how I feel he made me to live.

Discussion Questions

1. What do you think it means to live life fully?
2. What do you think about the phrase "living for yourself"?
3. Do you think you pay attention to life going on around you?
4. What do you think it means to feel God's pleasure?

conclusion

my thoughts on authenticity

SARAH

IN THE INTRODUCTION I spoke of my trip to India. Though I have been there several times since, that first visit as an adult will forever remain part of me. I didn't want to go there. India intimidated me. It seemed so foreign, and truthfully, far less comfortable than I liked. Being partly Indian and so therefore having been around people who had been to India before meant that I had heard many stories, and I wasn't at all sure I was up to the challenge. However, since this was the first opportunity I'd really had to go there, I couldn't very well turn it down. But I was afraid I would hate it, and that worried me for several reasons. The first one being that I was going to be there for two weeks, and if I hated it, two weeks seemed like an awfully long time. The other reason was that since my father was from there, I didn't want to hate it; I would have felt terribly guilty. But by the same token I didn't think I could tell my dad I didn't want to go to his country, and so I went with great trepidation.

When I stepped off the plane I immediately felt the dense air swallow me completely. India doesn't make tentative and polite introductions; rather she greets you by throwing her arms around you. I could feel it on my skin, smell it through my nose. I breathed India into my lungs. And I guess that's how it got inside me. I judged it all very quickly, as we so often do, and within twenty-four hours I decided that I kind of liked it and that I definitely could survive the next two weeks. And before the two weeks were complete, I was in love with the country. Yes, India is rich in culture, her people are beautiful and gracious, and I felt my senses fully engaged while there. And for all those reasons I loved it. But there was more. I know it sounds cliché, but I found a part of myself in India. I suppose that's not surprising, since India is literally in my blood. But it was surprising to me, shocking even. As a little girl growing up, I never embraced that part of my heritage, mostly because it was a little different, and I just wanted to blend in. Being biracial made this a little more difficult.

But there was a part of myself that awakened in India. Even now I can't exactly explain it except to say that I discovered things about myself that both surprised me and seemed strangely familiar at the same time, as though they had been hibernating. But that awakening fixed me on a trajectory of self-discovery that still continues as I both uncover more and fight to hang on to what I now know. I have learned that through knowing the person I am, I have also come to know my faith and know my God in a much richer way. I don't believe that, for me, it could have been any other way. And out of this process of discovery, though surely painful at times, came the idea for this book and the desire to grapple alongside others who are doing the same.

My mother read the Chronicles of Narnia to me when I was a little girl. Every night before bed she would read a chapter. Usually I would beg her to keep reading; the suspense was too great for me to wait until the next night to see what happened. Often she would oblige and read just one more chapter. Recently, a friend reminded me of this story. The character of Eustace Clarence Scrubb is first introduced in *The Voyage of the Dawn Treader*. Eustace is the cousin of Susan, Peter, Edmund, and Lucy, and he is a most unlikable boy. He is mean, stuck-up, and spoiled. And as the story progresses, the others grow more and more weary of Eustace. But then this cantankerous cousin is changed when he embarks on a most peculiar adventure. He wanders off from the group and finds himself face-to-face with a dragon. However, to his great luck, the dragon up and dies before Eustace's eyes. After raiding the lair, Eustace falls asleep. When he awakens some time later, he realizes that there is another dragon that has fallen asleep beside him.

With his exquisite storytelling flair, C. S. Lewis tells of how Eustace comes to realize that what he thought to be another dragon beside him is actually himself, his very own dragon limbs and claws. Of course, the boy's discovery that he is now in fact a monster in the flesh presents a number of problems. His digestive needs have changed, his culinary appetite has grown, and he is no longer able to speak. On the positive side, he is able to fly. But there is more; Eustace realizes he wants—and even needs—his friends whom he treated badly. He becomes very sorry for the way he has behaved, and as he grows to be more likable, even as a monster, he begins to like being liked. And then one night as Eustace lies awake, a grand and majestic lion approaches him.

It is Aslan, only Eustace doesn't know Aslan. The lion summons him to follow. He brings the dragon to a well that bubbles and gurgles and looks so inviting and refreshing. Eustace wants to jump in and swim, but Aslan tells him he will have to undress first. Of course, Eustace isn't wearing any clothes—I don't think dragons usually do. But he realizes that he can shed his scaly skin, thinking that must be what Aslan means. And so he begins to scratch at the scales, and his skin begins to peel off in one piece. I imagine it was like a snake shedding its skin, only much, much larger. And Eustace, seeing his skin lifeless on the ground, begins to walk toward the well. But as he goes to dip his toe in, he sees that once again his feet are scaly, and tough, still very dragonlike. Again he scratches off his scales, and again finds that though he removed his skin, there still remains a dragon skin underneath. Only after the third time does Aslan tell Eustace that he, the lion, will have to undress him. And so the lion swipes at Eustace with his giant paw.

And Eustace says, "The very first tear he made was so deep that I thought it had gone right into my heart."[16] But the lion continues to tear off the scaly skin, not seeming to take into account that Eustace is writhing in pain, crying out in agony as the dragon skin is ripped from him. When Aslan is finished, all that remains is the soft, pink skin of a boy—the dragon is no more. Then Aslan grabs Eustace and throws him into the pool, and though the water initially stings his fresh and delicate new skin, eventually the sting lessens and he feels the cool, refreshing water against his human skin. Finally, Aslan dresses him again, giving him new clothes, and now they are the clothes of a boy.

In many of the stories you have read, these women too have experienced the tearing off of their costume, or an outer layer of skin. Looking within yourself can be a frightening experience, but as a result these women have seen things in themselves that they never knew were there.

A lot of what these fifteen women wrestled with could be described as fear. We mask some of who we are because of fear. And it is like trying to win a battle without a full army. We need those strengths that God has given each one of us. But so often our strengths also become our weakness and our shame. We need to take it back, redeeming that strength, because after the pain of shedding the old layers, what remains is fresh and new skin.

It is sensitive skin too, susceptible to pain, and damages easily. But I believe that we are given new clothes to wear, although sometimes it seems like we are cleaning out our closets but then have nothing left to wear. We've discarded what we know we don't want, what no longer fits, but then we are left naked. A very wise woman cautioned me not to rush to put new clothes on. If we hurry to cover ourselves back up, often we end up with clothes that are ill-fitting once again. She advised that I be patient, that I be content with nothing in my closet for a while. In the Garden of Eden after Adam and Eve sinned, they too hurried to clothe themselves. But when God came along, he dressed them himself. To be still and wait for the new clothes can be as unnerving as shedding the old ones to begin with.

When I was working on the interviews for this book, there were times when I was completely overwhelmed. I saw so much of myself in many of the women that at times it was difficult to take notes. I wanted to be able to stop and think about what they were saying and how it was affecting me. In one woman I found a kindred voice in the present, in another I found confirmation about things I had been learning, and in another I felt as though I were glimpsing the future if I continued the path I was on. At times I felt overcome with all I was trying to process, and I began to think that this book was only for me, for my benefit, and not for others.

I began to wonder if God had led me down this journey of writing only for those moments of recognition and how they changed me. And maybe that's true in part, but it doesn't have to be the only truth. Maybe it was for me, but maybe it was for you too. At least that is my prayer. That you too have had those moments of recognition, that you've read words that startle you with their insight into your own heart, either in the past, present, or future. Because that has been the purpose all along—to find yourself somewhere along these stories. C. S. Lewis said, "Friendship is born at the moment when one person says to another, 'What? You too? I thought no one but myself . . .'"[17]

We need each other for more than just friendship. I don't think it takes any great mastery or influence to convince a woman that friends are important. But authenticity is important too. It's honesty with oneself and with each other that is so vital—and often so hard too. But why be honest? Aren't we only making ourselves more susceptible to judgment, disappointment, and hurt?

One woman I interviewed spoke of friendships from her past. When Mary Jane was young and newly married, she spent a great deal of time worrying about what others thought. When she and her husband moved to a city where they knew no one, they began going to a church in their area that was just getting off the ground. The church was small, and the women were very different from the type of woman she herself was, but also different from what she was used to. They didn't seem to worry about what other people thought, and they didn't seem to make much of an effort to impress others. When Mary Jane was invited to her first baby shower, she accepted and then was asked to bring food to it. She hadn't offered to do so and was taken aback by the request. "You want me to bring food?" she echoed back incredulously. The reply came back that, yes, everyone was expected to bring something.

Disdain immediately flashed across her mind when she thought of the hodgepodge of disorganized, disjointed culinary delight that awaited them all at the shower. This did not seem to be the type of baby shower she was used to, with diaper tower cakes, tiny tea sandwiches with the crusts cut off, and a repeating duck or little lamb theme. And it was true, these women didn't seem to worry very much about the cosmetic details, but what she discovered was that they were there for each other and supported each other in an authentic way.

One Sunday she was approached by a woman who asked her to join a small Bible study. They were to start the following week, and she was told only to bring a list of her goals. In her mind her only goal was a fresh manicure every week, so she felt a little out of place. When she arrived at the study there were three other women and a variety of ages. Mary Jane felt she didn't belong, and she was sure she had been invited to join only as the comic relief. But that study proved life changing, and not because of the study itself. The friendships she made there would forever stay with her, affecting the choices she would make and how she thought about life in the years to come, even many years after she moved away and lost touch with the women.

She found out a short time later that the study began because one woman was having marital problems. Her marriage counselor had advised her to gather a group of women together to find out what their stories of marriage were. The counselor hoped that she would gain perspective from hearing the experiences of others. And the women shared openly and authentically with each other, teaching Mary Jane about the immense value in being real and honest with each other. One morning when they all met together as they did every week, one woman shared candidly that she struggled with not feeling love toward her children at times. Mary Jane, having no children of her own, silently judged her, thinking what kind of a horrible woman wouldn't love her children even for a second. Many years later Mary Jane struggled with the same feelings, and her mind immediately returned to that day when another woman had the courage to be real and share her thoughts. And Mary Jane drew strength from that memory, even though it had been years ago, remembering that another woman had walked that path before her.

I also had the privilege of interviewing a group of women who were all very dear friends. I listened as each one shared and the others added to her story, often finishing each other's sentences, building each other up, even putting an arm around another when she became teary in her honesty. And I listened as they told of how they not only walked with each other in their dark days, but also grew spiritually together as God used their authenticity with each other to teach them more about themselves and his relationship to them.

And I think that though we say we want authentic relationships, they can be frightening. We judge each other so quickly, and we cut each other down in our judgments. And yet, we need each other just the same, and we need that authenticity, painful or not. At least I do. Because what I've found is this: if I am not honest with myself, if I am not willing to look deep within at that darkness that is there, then it stays there. If I can't go eye to eye with my weakness, and if I'm not truthful about it with myself, then my tendency is to hide it from others too. I pretend, I make excuses, I blame others—it's always someone else's fault. But then I have found myself going to God with the same attitude. I stand before God and make excuses. Sound familiar? It's been our way since the very beginning. After all, those are the exact same things Adam and Eve did in the garden.

My relationship with God is so often mirrored in my relationship with myself and with others. If I don't go deep with others, then I don't go deep with God. I just didn't see that truth when I didn't have the courage to look.

And there's another reason I think authenticity is necessary. We need those authentic relationships in order to live what we have learned with integrity. To live what you have come to know often requires great bravery, and we need each other to uphold that courage. As one of the women so beautifully said, "The strength is there, you just need relationships to pull it out of you."

And finally, I think we need authentic relationships to create space. Our fears, our shame, and our disappointments end up taking so much space within us. Like rising bread dough that doubles overnight, it often pushes out things that should be there. To be open with each other, to let people in, is just that—it is openness. And it acts like a puncture, an opening. I think of it much like a tracheotomy—which I only know about from shows like *ER*—though it can be painful, the tiny hole allows new breath to be taken in, and the air that needs to get out can be expelled as well.

You know the initial awkwardness when you're in a group of strangers and are required to interact? Having observed focus groups before, I find it fascinating to observe the group dynamics. The group will enter the room and be seated, and after brief instructions the moderator will begin to ask questions. But the group is nervous, and initially not forthcoming. They don't know each other, and that's as it should be for the purpose of the focus group. But there is always one person who is more talkative. And after that person gets the ball rolling, more participants are willing to speak up. They just need that icebreaker person.

So that's exactly what these brave women have done. They have broken the ice. They have stepped up, they have put themselves out there, and so now it is safe for you to do so too. Well, relatively safe. Because it's really not all that safe, is it? As I listened to story after story of these remarkable women, I saw many threads that wove us all together. As I noted earlier, one of them was fear. Everyone was afraid of something. To be real with yourself, to be real with others is actually pretty frightening. It certainly opens you up for judgment, for criticism, and as one of the women said, "for the world to confirm your lie." And then it feels like truth.

Self-discovery itself can make us fearful. But for me I came to a place where, as one woman poignantly described it, it was like childbirth. Once you start pushing that baby out, there's no pushing it back in. And that's the truth about self-discovery, about opening the door to those fears and choosing to fight them. There are times when it seems like it would be so much easier to retreat, to throw up the white flag and ask for permission to return to your old life. But I think it's almost a blessing that we come to a place where we are unable to do so. Because if we were, we certainly would, and then we would miss out on so much. If not for the pain we would miss out on seeing the way God brings you more into the person you are supposed to be so that he can use you.

And we are promised in Philippians 1:6 that "he who began a good work in you will carry it on until completion." Like the smoldering wick (Isa. 42:3), you will not be snuffed out. A wick smolders and dies because it lacks the properties within it to continue to burn. But, "a life truly lived burns away what is no longer relevant, gradually reveals our essence until at last we are strong enough to stand in our naked truth."[18]

notes

1. Dorothy Sayers, *The Human-Not-Quite-Human* (Grand Rapids: Eerdmans, 1971), 68.

2. Anne Lamott, *Traveling Mercies* (New York: Random House, 1999), 167.

3. Clarissa Pinkola Estes, *Women Who Run with the Wolves* (New York: Ballantine Books, 1992), 14.

4. Anne Lamott, *Bird by Bird* (New York: Anchor, 1995), 47.

5. Sayers, *The Human-Not-Quite-Human*, 68.

6. Paula Reeves, *Women's Intuition* (Boston: Conari Press, 1999), 5.

7. *Webster's Dictionary* (New Lanark, Scotland: Geddes and Grosset, 1995), 324.

8. Ruth A. Tucker, *God Talk* (Downer's Grove: InterVarsity Press, 2005), 12.

9. Ernest Jones, *Sigmund Freud: Life and Work*, vol. II (London: Hogarth Press, 1955).

10. W. H. Auden, "Age of Anxiety," *Collected Poems* (New York: Vintage International, 1976), 533.

11. Missy Stoddard, "Palm Beach Woman Sues Walgreen's," March 8, 2006, http://sun-sentinal.com.

12. Mary Pipher, *Reviving Ophelia* (New York: Ballantine Books, 1995), 170.

13. Linda Tschirhart Sanford and Mary Ellen Donovan, *Women and Self-Esteem* (New York: Penguin, 1984), 369.

14. Karen Horney, *Neurosis and Human Growth* (New York: W. W. Norton and Co., 1950), 65.

15. Ibid., 13.

16. C. S. Lewis, *The Voyage of the Dawn Treader* (New York: Harper Collins, 1952), 115.

17. C. S. Lewis, *The Four Loves* (New York: Harcourt Brace Jovanovich, 1960), 113.

18. Marion Woodman and Jill Mellick, *Coming Home to Myself* (Boston: Conari Press, 2000), 93.

Sarah Zacharias Davis is the director of marketing and events for Ravi Zacharias International Ministries and the author of *Confessions from an Honest Wife*. She graduated from Covenant College with a degree in education and lives in Atlanta, Georgia.

More Bible Studies from ℞ Revell

for individual or group use

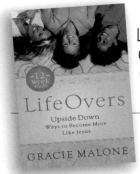

LifeOvers

Gain a greater understanding of the God who is in control, even when it doesn't feel like it.

Naked Fruit

Explore what it means to be like Christ, and discover how to display the fruit of the spirit in a way that's uniquely you. A MOPS book.

Breathe

Gentle, practical advice on how to make time for what matters most. Includes "breathing" exercises. A MOPS book.

Oxygen

A devotional that helps you take a deep breath for your soul, incorporating spiritual disciplines into your everyday life. A MOPS book.

Available at your local bookstore

What if we were

honest

with ourselves?

From sex to submission,
these women's stories
offer you real-life
encouragement . . .
to help you grow
deeper, more intimate
relationships.

confessions
from an
honest wife

on the mess,
mystery & miracle
of marriage

sarah zacharias davis